Are you a freak of nature?

Is the theory of evolution really true? Did all of the world's plants and animals grow out of a glob of primordial slime? Is man the mutant offspring of a hairy, belly-scratching, banana-belching baboon? In *From Goo to You by Way of the Zoo,* Harold Hill makes the evolutionists cringe by exposing the flaws and fallacies of the theory of evolution. In his spritely, enthusiastic style, he gives an eye-opening look into the mysteries of the world we live in. Using the basic rules of science to disprove evolution, Harold Hill demonstrates that the Bible's story of creation is the only scientifically possible origin of the species. He offers you amazing evidence that man was carefully engineered and constructed by a Supreme Architect. Harold Hill also shows that by following the instructions of the Manufacturer's Handbook—the Bible—we can overcome the effects and results of sin which has corrupted God's perfect creation. *From Goo to You by Way of the Zoo* will give you a hearty spiritual lesson on the true origin and nature of man and his relationship with his Creator.

BEST-SELLERS BY HAROLD HILL:

> *How to Live Like a King's Kid*
> *How to Be a Winner*
> *How to Live in High Victory*
> *Bible Answers for King's Kids*
> *How to Flip Your Flab—Forever*
> *How to Live the Bible Like a King's Kid*
> *God's in Charge Here*
> *The Money Book for King's Kids*
> *From Goo to You by Way of the Zoo*

If you don't have enough time for all the Bible reading you need to do, neither do I. That's why, everywhere I go, I listen to Bible tapes on a little cassette player. For ordering information about my favorite version, as well as about the books and teaching tapes that will help you with attitude control for victorious living, send a self-addressed stamped envelope to:

Harold E. Hill
King's Kids Korner
P.O. Box 8655
Baltimore, MD 21240
Phone: (301) 636-4518

From GOO to YOU by Way of the ZOO

HAROLD HILL with
Mary Elizabeth Rogers
and Irene Burk Harrell

Power Books

Fleming H. Revell Company
Old Tappan, New Jersey

Library of Congress Cataloging in Publication Data

Hill, Harold, date.
   From goo to you by way of the zoo.

   "Power books."
   Bibliography: p.
   1. Evolution—Religious aspects—Christianity.
2. Creation. 3. Nature—Religious aspects—Christianity.
4. Christian life—1960–   . I. Harrell, Irene Burk.
II. Rogers, Mary Elizabeth. III. Title,
BS659.H55   1985   231.7′65   84-11775
ISBN 0-8007-5174-4

Contents

5

TO the greatest folks in the world—
the young people of today.

Foreword

Apollo crews have visited the moon and returned safely to earth. Skylab astronauts have spent days working and living in space, and all have returned hale and hearty to earth.

Why are we flying to the moon? What is our purpose? What is the essential justification for the exploration of space? The answer, I am convinced, lies rooted not in whimsy, but in the nature of man.

Whereas all other living beings seem to find their places in the natural order and fulfill their role in life with a kind of calm acceptance, man clearly exhibits confusion. Why the anxiety? Why the storm and stress? Man really seems to be the only living thing uncertain of his role in the universe; and in his uncertainty, he has been calling since time immemorial upon the stars and the heavens for salvation and for answers to his eternal questions: Who am I? Why am I here?

Astronomy is the oldest science, existed for thousands of years as the only science, and is today considered the queen of the sciences. Although man lacks the eye of the night owl, the scent of the fox, or the hearing of the deer, he has an uncanny ability to learn about abstruse things like the motions of planets, the cradle-to-the-grave cycle of the stars, and the distance between stars.

The mainspring of science is curiosity. There have always been men and women who felt a burning desire to know what was under the rock, beyond the hills, across the oceans. This restless breed now wants to know what makes an atom work, through what process life reproduces itself, or what is the geological history of the moon.

But there would not be a single great accomplishment in the history of mankind without faith. Any man who strives to accomplish something needs a degree of faith. But many people find the churches, those old ramparts of faith, badly battered by the onslaught of three hundred years of scientific skepticism. This has led many to believe that science and religion are not compatible, that "knowing" and "believing" cannot live side by side.

Nothing could be further from the truth. Science and religion are not antagonists. On the contrary, they are sisters. While science tries to learn more about the creation, religion tries to better understand the Creator.

Many men who are intelligent and of good faith say they cannot visualize God. Well, can a physicist visualize an electron? The electron is materially inconceivable and yet we use it to illuminate our cities, guide our airliners through the night skies, and take the most accurate measurements. What strange rationale makes some physicists accept the electron as real while refusing to accept God? I am afraid that, although they really do not understand the electron either, they are ready to accept it because they managed to produce a rather clumsy mechanical model of it borrowed from rather limited experience in other fields, but they wouldn't know how to begin building a model of God.

For me the idea of a creation is inconceivable without God. One cannot be exposed to the law and order of the universe without concluding that there must be a divine intent behind it all.

Some evolutionists believe that the creation is the result of a random arrangement of atoms and molecules over billions of years. But when they consider the development of the human brain by random processes within a time span of less than a million years, they have to admit that this span is just not long enough. Or take the evolution of the eye in the animal world. What random process could possibly explain the simultaneous evolution of the eye's optical system, the nervous conductors of the optical signals from the eye to the brain, and the optical nerve center in the brain itself where the incoming light impulses are converted to an image the conscious mind can comprehend?

Our space ventures have been only the smallest of steps in the vast reaches of the universe and have introduced more mysteries than they have solved. Speaking for myself, I can only say that the grandeur of the cosmos serves to confirm my belief in the certainty of a Creator.

Of course, the discoveries in astronomy, biology, physics, and even in psychology have shown that we have to enlarge the medieval image of God. If there is a mind behind the immense complexities of the multitude of phenomena which man, through the tools of science, can now observe, then it is that of a Being tremendous in His power and wisdom. But we should not be dismayed by the relative insignificance of our own planet in the vast universe as modern science now sees it. In fact God deliberately reduced Himself to the stature of humanity in order to visit the earth in person, because the cumulative effect over the centuries of millions of individuals choosing to please themselves rather than God had infected the whole planet. When God became a man Himself, the experience proved to be nothing short of pure agony. In man's time-honored fashion, they would unleash the whole arsenal of weapons against Him: misrepresentation, slander, and accusation of treason. The stage was set for a situation without parallel in the history of the earth. God would visit creatures and they would nail Him to the cross!

Although I know of no reference to Christ ever commenting on scientific work, I do know that He said, "Ye shall know the truth, and the truth shall make you free." Thus I am certain that, were He among us today, Christ would encourage scientific research as modern man's most noble striving to comprehend and admire His Father's handiwork: The universe as revealed through scientific inquiry is the living witness that God has indeed been at work.

When astronaut Frank Borman returned from his unforgettable Christmas, 1968, flight around the moon with Apollo 8, he was told that a Soviet Cosmonaut recently returned from a space flight had commented that he had seen neither God nor angels on his flight. Had Borman seen God? the reporters inquired. Frank Borman replied, "No, I did not see Him either, but I saw His evidence."

WERNHER VON BRAUN

Foreword

It was 1961. I had just graduated from test-pilot school and considered myself one of the "hottest" pilots in the sky. One morning as I was flying with a student in a light aircraft, we crashed. The plane did not burn, but we were seriously injured—broken legs, broken jaw, many teeth gone, concussion, multiple lacerations.

When I awakened in the hospital, doctors told me I probably would not fly again. You can imagine my despair.

I cried out to God, "Why did this happen to me?"

As I lay in the hospital, I had much time to pray—for understanding and for healing. I knew God loved me, and He made it possible for me to fly again.

My love for going fast and high led me into the space program. Already I had been trained as an engineer, technician, pilot, and test pilot. In the astronaut program, we were taught about the geology of the earth so we could relate to the features we would see on the moon. In that training, I was told for the first time that the earth was 4 or 5 billion years old. There was a long discussion of the fossil record, indicating a very old earth. We were taught about evolution.

Evolution. What did it mean? You mean the earth evolved? You mean I evolved from something like an ape?

Never having had any courses in high school or college on the subject, I had never given evolution much thought before 1971. I assumed that our professors believed what they were teaching, but I never asked them about their beliefs. Eager to have a chance to fly in space and, I hoped, to reach the moon, I didn't want to rock the boat.

As you know, I made the flight. When we left the earth, we carried a microfilmed copy of a prayer covenant, signed by the people in my church who were praying for our safety and the success of our mission.

I felt very special when I looked down at my footprints on the moon. The scientists had told me they would be there for a million years. Looking up, I could see the earth, like a beautiful blue marble in the sky. It was so far away, and yet I felt strangely at home on the moon.

The days I spent there were very exciting—because God was there. I could feel His presence. In difficult times, I prayed and His answer was immediate. I was inspired to quote Psalms 121:1: "I will lift up mine eyes unto the hills, from whence cometh my help." I knew my help was coming from the Lord who made the heavens and the earth. I knew He made the moon, and He made it possible for Jim Irwin to place his footprints there.

God guided us to the discovery of a white rock gleaming in the sunlight and almost free from dust. It was lifted up, sitting on another rock, and seemed to be saying, "Here am I. Take me." The press called it "Genesis Rock."

When our mission returned to earth, I thanked the men who designed and built our spacecraft, those who helped to operate the systems during the flight, fellow Americans and dear friends around the world who had prayed for the success of our trip. Most of all, I thanked God for allowing us to leave the earth and explore a portion of His heavens.

The beautiful Blue Planet is unique in all the universe. As far as we know, it is the only natural home for man. God made this perfect place just for us. Could anything as extraordinary as the earth have just evolved? It is not very probable.

We have learned so much about life, the earth, and our universe. No matter where we look, whether it is microscopic or macroscopic, we see design. I believe it is divine design.

Everything on earth is in harmony, the result of God's creation. I came back from space with new appreciation for the earth, for life, and for the Lord. I came back believing that evolution is just a theory—and a preposterous one at that.

I have known the Lord almost all my life, having committed my life to Him when I was only eleven years old. For many years I was a "silent" Christian. It was only after my return to earth that I realized the importance of a spiritual dimension to life. Without it, you have nothing.

Jesus asked, "For what shall it profit a man, if he shall gain the whole world, and lose his own soul?" (Mark 8:36). I know that man can go to the moon and return to earth in deep despair unless he knows the Son. I rededicated my life to Christ because I knew He had blessed our journey into space.

I believe Jesus Christ walking on the earth is more important than man walking on the moon. Just as surely as He walked two thousand years ago, He wants to walk today in your life. All you have to do is call upon Him. He wants you to have life and have it more abundantly (*see* John 10:10). The first step of entering into this abundant life is to acknowledge your need of a Saviour. Your first prayer might be, "Lord, help me a sinner." Then invite Him into your life by faith. Jesus said, "I am the way, the truth, and the life: no man cometh unto the Father, but by me" (John 14:6).

I pray that as you read these words, you will yield your life to the Master and let Him guide your footprints forever.

The flight medallions carried by Apollo 15 bore the inscription, "Man's flight through life is sustained by the power of his knowledge." Now I know that my flight through life has been sustained by the power of my knowledge of Jesus Christ.

I have viewed the earth as God Himself must view it, and I will never be the same.

COLONEL JAMES B. IRWIN, ASTRONAUT
President, High Flight Foundation

In 1972, Colonel Irwin founded High Flight Foundation, an interdenominational Christian Foundation dedicated to sharing the Good News that "God walking on earth is more important than man walking on the moon."

For further information about this ministry, contact:
High Flight Foundation
Box 1387
Colorado Springs, CO 80901

Opus Gloppus

or

The Rhyme of the Ancient-est Mariner

Proto Zoan is my name—
  just call me "Little Proto."
I'm sorry that I have no proof—
  not even a passport photo—
of my beginning back in time,
  when from a glob of goo,
supposedly I started things
  from goo——to zoo—to *you*!

For untold centuries I thought
  that all was going well—
then I became dissatisfied
  as just a single cell.
My knowledge of genetics
  soon stood me in good stead:

by mutational progression
    I'd become a quadruped.

As every Little Proto knows
    there's lots of room for doubt
that accidental happenings
    can bring such things about,
but here is where blind faith comes in—
    belief in the absurd—
that simple Little Proto
    could evolve to soaring bird.

Not in a single step, of course,
    these things take many years—
eternity is just one cog
    in evolution's gears.
Ambition surged within my cell
    down in my gloppy bog:
by protozoan effort
    I'd become a pollywog.

For umpteen million years or so
    I wogged my way about,
powered by my groovy tail
    till fins began to sprout.
Or was it scales I next acquired?
    Really, I forget—
with evolution in control
    You don't know what you'll get!

You needn't take my word for it—
    one guess is like another—

but stick around and I will prove
    you are a monkey's brother.
Brace up your credibility
    if things seem slow to change—
we deal, you know, with time and chance,
    and sometimes things are strange.

Another million years went by—
    or maybe three or four—
and I sprang from my puddle
    and splatted on the shore.
Now please do not embarrass me
    with questions such as this:
"Where did you swap your gills for lungs?
    You said you were a fish!"

Years later, in a flighty mood
    one prehistoric morn
I gave a great leap forward—
    full feathered and airborne!
I landed in a treetop
    where I kept on evolving
though one remaining problem
    was superslow dissolving.

Evolutionary changes
    are supposed to benefit,
but, oh! my droopy, stupid tail
    did just the opposite.
It tangled in the underbrush,
    it slithered through the muck.
My mutational monstrosity
    was nothing but bad luck!

It blistered in the noonday sun,
    it mildewed in the rain;
if I could just be shed of it,
    I'd lose a major pain.
My patient waiting bore much fruit
    as happens without fail;
I changed into a reeking ape
    with teeth and hair and—tail.

As such I wondered sometimes
    while ages came and went:
this monkey-business way of life—
    could it all be accident?
Daily my wonderings mounted
    and my ponderings increased:
Was preacher Darwin really right?
    Could man descend from beast?

Oh, it was fun to be an ape—
    I loved to swing in trees.
It was great to munch bananas
    and such fun to scratch my fleas.
I howled with all my comrades
    and I gibbered at the moon
suspecting that in due time
    my carefree days were doomed.

Could I recode my DNA—
    change it drastically—
and so become a humanoid
    instead of chimpanzee?
Peoplehood filled all my dreams
    but first my tail must go

by freaking out my gene pool
    for a million years or so.

The million years went swiftly past
    and soon a million more
and then one day I noticed that
    my tail was feeling sore!
My tail dropped off, my fur grew thin—
    Old Darwin strikes again!
From happy, jolly simian
    I *would* become a man!

As soon as I had shed that tail
    I stood upright, and whee!
My peoplehood was coming fast—
    just you wait and see.
One day I shaved my fur off—
    quite becoming, I would say,
and from there to hairless apehood
    took but an eon day.

Acquired characteristics
    are not inherited—ever?
To fit within genetics' laws,
    I was extremely clever:
I trained my wife and wee ones
    to confess their tails weren't there
and one day while they waited
    their tails vanished in thin air!

As soon as they had shed their tails,
    they stood upright like me.

Behold us, homo sapiens—
　　our whole family.
But I'm not quite sure I like it
　　now that I'm a man.
Come to spend a day with me
　　and I'll show you what I can.

Look into my mirror
　　while I shave to go to work.
Go with me to the kitchen
　　while I put coffee on to perk.
　Climb into my auto,
　　we'll fight traffic to my job,
elevator to the top floor
　　and elbow through the mob.

Be bored with me through conferences,
　　sweat when the market dives.
Join me in a briefcase lunch,
　　watch pressure give me hives.
Life's so tough I'm in a daze
　　I hate this stress and strife.
From here I don't know where to go
　　Is this all there is to life?

How I've longed for Proto days—
　　Man, that was really livin'!
No work, no tax, no traffic jams—
　　Proto life was heaven.
Nothing to do but just be me—
　　all day to ooze around—
returning to those good ole days
　　is the neatest "out" I've found.

If evolution is a fact
   then it will never quit.
I'm researching the subject now—
   what will become of it?
The findings of my studies
   I have not yet divulged
but the title of my thesis is
   "When Proto Comes Unbulged."

I'll give you just a hint or two
   of what my study's finding:
With prices climbing up and up
   and ecologists reminding
that this old universe is doomed
   unless we cease from strife,
folks are wondering if they can
   revert to Proto life.

Evolving backward ought to be
   a cinch compared to climbing
since on our team is entropy,
   which guarantees declining.
Becoming just a blob again
   "to a T" would suit me.
How to get there is a cinch—
   doing what comes naturally.

Let's retro-volve our people cells
   returning whence we came—
in time, we can do anything
   in evolution's game.
Farewell, my fellow anthropoids,
   until we meet back yonder—

a pair of blobs in globs of goo
   without a care to ponder.

So long, farewell, *auf wiedersehen,*
   I'm headed back in time.
That carefree life I used to have
   will soon again be mine.
I'll see you then in goo-land
   if my eyes don't disappear.
If we're both blind, I'll bump you—
   to let you know I'm near.

But I'll bump you very carefully
   there'll be no jostling pace
to start a new mutation
   relaunching this whole mad race.

Have you perhaps detected gaps
   of credibility
as we've progressed from freak to freak
   up and down our family tree?
Apparently a Ph.D.
   without the word of God
will blithely buy the biggest lie—
   if it's the evolution fraud.

The Piltdown man and all his clan
   long proven just a hoax
are taught as fact by eggheads
   with psychopathic boasts.
How so-called brains could be misled
   by evolution's trick
is answered in Isaiah 1:
   "The whole head is sick!"

Apparently the EIB*
   has robbed the human race
of choice between a naked ape
   and a God of saving grace.
Else why is theory pushed as fact
   in higher education
rejecting with a tight-closed mind
   the Creator's account of creation?

But before you start unhappening
   from man to protozoan
via chimp and bird and fish and wog
   to the goo where you first got goin',
heed God's urgent warning
   against phony scientists.**
He must have known that Darwin's dream
   would be our nemesis.

Can you believe life started out
   as carefree globs of goo,
evolved from fish to bird to ape
   and ended up as you?
The theory is, as theories go,
   rather odd and fakey.
The truth, however, is a lot
   more sturdy and not shaky.

The viable alternative
   is worth consideration:
Whodunit? *could* be answered best
   by biblical creation
Where in six days God made the world
   and everything therein,

including man, His masterpiece,
   for fellowship with Him.

Divergent as these concepts are
   concerning mankind's start,
forget Egghead Foolosophy
   and let yourself get smart.
It's time to wise up, open your eyes up
   to the possibility
That a God who cares, to us declares,
   "I love *you*—why not trust ME?"

Take heart, dear reader, and read on—
   you'll find the whole true story
in which there's rather less of goo
   and rather more of glory.

*EIB: Educated Idiot Box. For full details on the EIB, read *How to Live Like a King's Kid* (Plainfield, N.J.: Bridge Publishing Company).
**1 Timothy 6:20.

1

First Things First

In the beginning—WHAT?

    Evolution says—Goo.

    The Bible says—God.

Does evolution really provide the answer?

Did we actually descend from freak apes?

Were our beginnings in a sea of chemical soup?

Or in a cloud of hot gases?

And if so, where did the soup or the gases come from?

Or is it just possible that a Supreme Being—God Himself—carefully engineered and created the whole show?

These are some of the questions I began asking a few years ago when I suddenly realized that what had started out as soft-headed theory—the theory of evolution—was being taught as hard fact.

It had always seemed rather weird to me that so-called scientists were willing to pin their hopes on the ramblings of a religious dreamer (Darwin's only degree was in theology) to the exclusion of all other possible alternatives. A true scientist always welcomes conflicting ideas and alternative theories, because he's looking for the truth. In this, the evolutionist does not measure up; he reveals himself as a phony scientist by having a mind that is tightly closed to any facts foreign to his beliefs. He is unteachable—a sure sign of insecurity, uncertainty, and unscientific-ness.

My business is science. Scientists who do it for money are called engineers. My clients expect me to produce results, and so do I. Therefore, I cannot afford to settle for less than the most authoritative answer available; I can't afford to overlook any possible theory.

After several decades of one-sided, so-called scientific brainwashing, I decided to investigate for myself what the available evidence reveals about the whole matter of where we came from and where we're going. My search began in real earnest the day I received a book entitled *The Harmony of Science and Scripture,* by Dr. Harry Rimmer, one of the foremost scientists of this century. It came to me from his widow with a note saying she was praying for another scientist—me—to carry on the work on which her husband had spent many years—the work of acquainting the world with all the facts concerning the true story of our beginnings so we could get out from under the deadly dogmatism of the evolutionists and make up our own minds about the start-up of things.

As you begin to consider my report, it will be helpful for you to look at a few definitions and some foundation facts:

First of all, just what do we mean when we say a thing is scientific? What is the difference between science and religion? And where does philosophy come in?

To eliminate a lot of confusion about these things, let's examine some basic principles. True science never dogmatically says things will happen in the future just the way they did in the past. It simply says that based on past performance of a system, it may be assumed that we can expect similar events to occur in the future.

For example, let's perform experiment A in which we instruct a small boy to toss a ball into the air five hundred times while we keep a careful record of what happens to the ball. If things go according to our expectations, the ball will fall exactly as many times as it is tossed into the air.

If we need more statistical evidence, we might instruct the small boy to repeat his part of the experiment another one thousand times. Now our record will probably show that the ball has fallen fifteen hundred times out of fifteen hundred tosses. Then we can feel reasonably safe in writing the Law of the Falling Ball:

> Based on statistical evidence gathered by experimentation, a ball, when tossed into the air by a small boy, will fall to earth or into the hands of the tosser. However, be it noted that we cannot guarantee this will happen in the future, because we have never observed the future in operation. Our supposition is based purely on what we have observed in the past.

True science deals only with things that are:

1. Observable. They can be seen in action.
2. Repeatable. They can be caused to happen again and again under proper conditions.
3. Interrelated. All systems are related to each other. Mathematics never calls physics a liar. Chemistry never bad-mouths thermodynamics. Electrical technology has never been caught ridiculing the Law of the Lever.

In other words, a scientist is someone who deals with the real world in the "right now" of human existence. Furthermore, a true scientist uses two methods of approaching any situation:

1. The statistical approach, based on past happenings.
2. The intuitive approach, based on feelings, hunches, and educated guesses.

Statistics are essential to most scientific investigations and to the resulting so-called laws or principles, which don't require anything of anybody but merely explain how things have been observed to work. For instance, the Law of Gravity doesn't prevent anyone from jumping off the top of a high building; it simply says that, based on statistical evidence, jumping off a high roof invariably produces lumps somewhere in the anatomy of the jumper.

The Law of the Highway Speed Limit doesn't prevent anyone from traveling faster than the posted speed. It merely says, "If we catch you at it, we have ways and means of making you wish you hadn't done it."

In the same way, the laws of our earth sciences simply make it possible to predict, with some degree of certainty, what will probably take place under given conditions. There are no guarantees though. In my own profession of electrical engineering, I can predict with great accuracy just what will happen in a power circuit under various conditions. But you don't need my engineering degree to learn that electricity will jolt your back teeth if you stick your finger into a turned-on light socket. You created your own statistical evidence the first time you tried it. At least I did.

Remember, a law demands nothing of anybody, it simply describes how a system works, based on what has happened in the past. A true scientist never dogmatically says, "What I have observed in the past guarantees identical behavior in the future." Statistics form a fairly reliable base for predicting the future, but it's never a sure thing.

So much for the statistical approach. The intuitive approach is important too. A long time ago when I was taking college physics, Dr. Albert Einstein's theory of relativity was much discussed. The theory, expressed in a mathematical formula, is $E = mc^2$. In the formula, E = energy, m = mass, and c = the speed of light. Among other things, the theory says that energy and matter are interchangeable at the speed of light multiplied by itself. Popular belief at the time was that it couldn't be done. Einstein's theory was strictly intuitive—but it turned out to be right.

We proved it with the atom bomb.

Now, how does religion differ from science? Does religion have to be repeatable, observable, and interrelated? No, religion is not limited by any boundaries. It doesn't even need any "evidence." Religion is simply a head trip, entered into at any time by anyone, for any particular purpose—or for no purpose at all. It's one's chosen way of thinking about things, based solely on the what a person believes. Philosophy is just another name for religion—not for science.

Since the origin of the earth and of all life is neither observable nor repeatable—that is, we didn't see it, and we can't make it happen again—we can't come to any "scientific" decision about it. But we can examine all possible evidence and form our own religious or philosophical conclusions.

Now that we have some yardstick principles and definitions to go with, we're ready for a look at the evidence for our religious or philosophical beliefs about the origin of the little corner of the universe called planet earth. But first, what is *evidence*? According to my dictionary, *evidence* is "grounds for belief, indication, sign, bearing witness."

Remember, on the subject of evolution versus creation, there is absolutely no conclusive proof on either side. But there is plenty of evidence in what we can observe and in what science has learned about its behavior. Let's examine it now with an open mind, and you can make your own decision about how you got here.

To sum it all up: Science deals only with the present observable, repeatable, interrelated happenings on planet earth in the present "now" of human existence. A scientist is operating on the level of religion or philosophy when he tells you that the earth is a billion years old. He's entitled to that opinion—religion is a personal matter—but he can't call it science, because it doesn't fit the criteria.

And now, on with the search as we examine together the evidence furnished by the evolutionist on the one hand and the Bible and the *true science* on the other. At the end, make your own decision on the question *How did it all begin?*

From goo to you by way of the zoo?

or

By a special act of creation by a loving heavenly Father
who created you and me in His image and likeness?

Evolution says—Goo.
The Bible says—God.
What will you say?

2

How Did It All Begin?

Phony Scientists' Theories

Ever since man began, he has wondered about himself. "Where did I come from?" "How did I get here?" And he has tried to come up with a concept of the beginning of things that would satisfy his understandable insatiable curiosity.

When I was a boy, there was a theory that mice "just happened" when a pile of rags was left in a corner of the attic. "Spontaneous generation," the old folks called it. In much the same way, people believed that pond water produced frogs, and that meat left in the open air generated maggots.

Then someone began studying maggots and found they were offspring of flies that had laid eggs on the surface of the meat. Covering the meat put an end to maggot production.

When the microscope came along and revealed the presence of all kinds of organisms invisible to the naked eye, many scientists believed at first that the organisms resulted from spontaneous generation in the same way as the mice in the attic, frogs in ponds, and maggots on meat. They based their belief on the fact that anything left exposed to open air soon became contaminated with millions of microorganisms.

Then along came Louis Pasteur to upset all the theories based on ignorance. He proved by experiment that the tiny organisms actually "rode in" on airborne dust particles. This new light about an old fact eventually put an end to the spontaneous generation theory in that area of observable scientific phenomena.

Today any scientist who still believed in the spontaneous generation theory about microorganisms would be laughed off the face of the earth for his ignorance. But in the area of speculation about the much broader question, "How did planet earth and all that dwells therein get here?" the spontaneous generation folks are still with us. They're the ones who push the theory that the universe began with a huge *bang* when a giant cloud of red-hot gases exploded out in space. After the explosion, these unenlightened folks tell us, the gases condensed into the solid matter we have today.

But a basic law of physics says that hot gases continue to expand in space as long as no restriction interferes with such expansion. If you'll check any high school physics book, you'll find that hot gases never condense to form solid matter.

"But how about when gases cool?" someone's asking. "Some of them form solids then, don't they?" Sure, gases can cool, assuming conditions are right for the transfer of the heat energy to another place. And if the gas happens to be CO_2—carbon dioxide—you can even get a hunk of dry ice out of the deal. But there's a catch. For an exploding gas to cool, the laws of physics say there would have to be something cooler to receive the heat energy. Heat can't be dissipated into nothing; it has to flow downhill—from the hotter something to the cooler something.

This presents a big problem for the "Big Bang" evolutionists. If there was nothing in the universe prior to the bang incident, the state of nothingness that existed could hardly be considered a suitable medium for the transfer of energy. "Nothing" can do nothing about anything. There'd be no way for the cloud to go about cooling off.

And where would the heat—which is a high level of energy—come from in the first place? Did it just "happen" like mice in the attic? And what kind of intelligence brought together all the elements necessary to produce life billions of years after the whole mess exploded? Why would a conglomeration of dust particles, coming from a no-dust environment, suddenly get together and pool their individual energy quanta to blow each other away? Can you find any reason to believe that such an arrangement would ever appear out of the nothing that preceded it? I can't. In the world where I live, dust results from the wearing away of something. In a universe completely empty of anything that could show wear, where did the dust particles come from to form that cloud in the first place?

After considering the questions that naturally arise, there is no way anyone of reasonable intelligence can follow the unreasoning of the Big Bang theory with a straight face. And that's not the only theory around that just can't hold water. Let's look for a moment at the theory proposed by another group of scientists, who say that all life began in a chemical soup caused by a bolt of lightning billions of years ago.

Once upon a time, a researcher named Sidney Fox decided to check out this theory. In his "origin of life" experiment, a mixture of amino acids is boiled for several hours, cooled, mixed with water, and filtered. After the mixture cools, an accumulation of glop settles out, which the author fondly calls "protenoid microspheres." The glop is actually an assortment of polymers or amino acid chains. Referring to them as "protocells," Fox claims the microspheres are similar to living cells in that they multiply by division.

For Fox's theory to work, the atmosphere would have to be

composed exclusively of swamp gas, deadly carbon monoxide, carbon dioxide, ammonia, nitrogen, hydrogen, and water. Since the atmosphere of earth is actually composed chiefly of carbon dioxide, nitrogen, oxygen, and water, the theory would strike out without ever getting to first base.

Furthermore, at the extremely high temperature that would be required to trigger cell evolution under this theory—a temperature far above the boiling point of water—complete destruction of the raw material of unknown origin would take place. This seems not to bother the proponents of the theory, however. Making up the rules as they go along, they glibly explain, "Well, it probably all took place on the edge of a volcano, and a friendly rainstorm just happened to come along in the nick of time to cool things off before the heat got fatal."

To me the soup isn't the only thing cooled off in the explanation. As I look at it, the whole argument isn't so hot, but it *is* full of holes.

Just where did they find that mixture of completely pure amino acids in the first place? Such a conglomeration doesn't appear in nature but must be refined in a modern laboratory in order to be used in the experiment. A mixture containing even a micropart of any of the great variety of other chemical compounds found on the primordial earth would have rendered the boiling fruitless. What is the statistical probability of a supply of pure amino acids occurring in nature, even without the high temperature conditions that would quickly destroy the acids anyhow? A big fat zero.

At its best, the Fox theory is so full of holes as not to warrant serious consideration as the possible start-up basis of all life. But if the idea is intriguing to you, you have my permission to pursue it further in the books that have been written on the subject by Dr. Duane T. Gish and published by the Institute for Creation Research, San Diego, CA 92116. If you think that

Dr. Gish's writing is designed to persuade you that the Fox theory is valid, you've got another think coming.

So much for Mr. Fox and his cohorts. Through the centuries, there have been many other theories about where life began. Let's explore some of them.

The ancient Egyptians said their god created the Nile River. In the banks of the Nile were little white fishbait worms. There were no other creatures on earth at that time, and one day their supreme god became lonely. He decided to invent people so he would have somebody to talk to. To accomplish his purpose, he sent a flood which washed the little white worms out of the mudbank. Lo and behold, once they got their feet on the ground, they turned into men and women. Their god wasn't lonely anymore. He had plenty of people to play with and talk to.

The ancient Babylonians had a different idea. Their supreme god, Marduk, got lonely one day, too, and started dreaming up a way to have companionship. When he had dreamed long enough, he took action, puckered up, and spat upon the earth he had created. Wherever his spit lit, a man sprang up. It was a good game, so he invited the men to join him.

"Go and do likewise," Marduk said. "Make me some more people." The men got in the act, spat, and women sprang up from their spittle. Not to be left out, the women got busy, too, and the rest of creation came into being. Everything that was made was made from slobber. Not very romantic, but it beat being lonesome.

Much later, a theologian named Charles Darwin took an extended trip on the good ship *Beagle* as an amateur naturalist. The voyage lasted for five years—up and down the coast of South America, to many islands, and around the world. When he wasn't being seasick, Darwin acted like a modern Snoopy, looking into things. He practiced birdwatching, and collected a whole bunch of free samples of plants, animals, rocks, and fossils and sent them home to merrie England.

Upon his return, he stirred all the specimens around in his mind for years and years, read a few books about nature, and came up with a whole Pandora's box full of ideas, right out of his very own head. Darwin theorized that all forms of life were kissing cousins, that every living thing had descended from a common ancestor, species continually improving themselves, the weak members dying out, those fit to live surviving, the sexiest multiplying faster than the others.

The biggest bombshell of his unbiblical imaginings was that man was a direct descendant of a reeking, itching, jungle baboon. Well, almost. In his *Descent of Man,* Darwin wrote:

> We do not know whether man is descended from some small species, like the chimpanzee, or from one as powerful as the gorilla.

Either way, chimp or gorilla, Darwin made a monkey out of himself, and evolutionists have been making monkeys out of themselves ever since.

Now Darwin didn't pretend to be a scientist to start with. He had dropped out of med school after two years of it. Furthermore, Darwin never claimed his theory of evolution was a fact, and he was rather surprised to find that he had unintentionally invented a new religion.

For some strange reason, even though they knew no one could ever prove Darwin's theory,[1] some so-called scientists chose to believe in evolution instead of believing God's own account of how things began. These "evolutionists" got their heads together and agreed upon a new "history" of the origin of intelligent life on earth. (Of course, they never bothered to explain where the unintelligent life came from that furnished the raw ingredients to start the whole thing. They didn't because they couldn't.)

Once upon a time, they said, about 4.5 billion years ago, there was a simple little cell wriggling in a swamp. (There's no such thing as a simple little cell. The single cell is one of the most complex mechanisms imaginable, but evolutionists choose to ignore that fly in their ointment.) For practically forever, the evolutionists said, the little protozoan just wriggled happily around, humming to itself in the primordial ooze, because it didn't know anything better to do. There were no Joneses to keep up with in those days, taxes were nonexistent, and it didn't *need* anything more than singing and dancing to keep itself happy.

It was a good thing little Proto was satisfied with so little for so long, because evolution requires practically forever before the least little thing can happen. If there is a god in their system, he has to be a powerless god who can't do anything but sit back and twiddle his thumbs, waiting for nature to take its course.

Well, eventually, after millions of years, the protozoan—and the thumb-twiddling god—were rewarded for their patience. Nature finally got around to taking its course, and the little wriggling protozoan discovered something new. There were bumpy places sticking out on its sides! It had lumps!

None of the rest of the family had sprouted such adornments; little Proto had graduated to something all by himself, with no ancestral precedents to guide him. What an exciting time it was!

Everybody flocked around to observe these fascinating bulges for a few more million years—after all, there was no television, no wide-screen movies, and they had to watch *something*.

And then one day, little Proto woke up earlier than anybody

else, looked lovingly down at his exclusive bulges, and saw that they had been turned into fins while he slept. Magically, though he had never seen such things before, he knew just what to do with them. He woke up the whole community with his gurgling shouts of joy.

"Hey, Ma! Look! I got fins! I'm a fish! Watch me swim!" How did he know he was a fish? Search me. Meanwhile, swim he did. Instead of just lying there in the same place all day long, slithering around in circles, little Proto shifted into high gear and swam off in search of adventure. He must have found a girl friend somewhere who liked his credentials, because after a while, the waters teemed with finned swimmers, lording it over the protozoans who hadn't grown lumps.

"Wait a minute!" someone's hollering. "Acquired characteristics can't be passed on genetically."

Shhh! I know it, but don't let the evolutionists hear you say that. It'll spoil their theory.

There is another catch, too. In order for a structure to change, something must act upon it from outside to change the genetic coding of the cell. Changing the genetic coding of a cell is nothing simple, nothing that can be done with a hairpin and Scotch tape. It's a big deal, like reprogramming a fantastically complex computer. Besides that, scientists have long observed that any genetic change or mutation that sets in will destroy it sooner or later.

A mutation always represents an increase in disorder, is often sterile, and invariably a mutant is less able to cope with its surroundings than its parent was. That means that the protozoan that grew lumps would have bowed out by the second generation, simply because mutants can't make it. There is no way that a mutant could multiply and replenish the earth.

But evolutionists can't be bothered with such observable facts as these. Their minds are made up. Facts just confuse the issue. And so the evolutionist outwits the facts by writing his own rules as he goes along. Real scientists know that mutants usually die out, so the evolutionist authors a new *un*scientific rule which proclaims, "Mutants live longer because they are an improvement." If you ask him to name a single example, you'll have a long wait. There simply isn't any such animal.

But in the evolutionist's make-believe world, the impossible new, improved protozoan with fins swims about happily until one day, after a few million more years, he notices some new lumps. They're on the bottom of him this time, not on the sides. Once again, he knows exactly what they're for.

"Hey, Dad, look! I got legs! I can walk!"

He staggers up onto the land, and lo and behold, he's a lizard.

But how can he breathe? Where'd he get lungs all of a sudden?

Don't ask me, ask the evolutionist who dreamed the whole thing up. He'll tell you the protozoan got lungs in the same place he got legs:

"He evolved them."

Anyhow, the protozoan-turned-fish has become a leaping lizard, romping around the landscape. And he has a ball for a few million years.

And then one day—you guessed it—history repeats itself, and he gets lumpy again. No, it's not adolescent acne, it's too far back for that, it must be—wings!

"Hey, man, watch out! With these things, I oughta be able to take off and fly."

He backs up to get a running start, but he can't seem to get it off the ground. And for millions of years, he's a menace to navigation. His monstrous winglike appendages get in everybody's way, and he falls all over himself, a big clumsy lizard with wings that won't work. But he's persistent as all get out. In his frustration, he flaps his wings so hard and long one day, they begin to fray along the edges.

"Eureka, Dad! Feathers!"

Where'd the lizard get such a crazy idea as to think he could fly in the first place? Why, from his study of the principles of aerodynamics, that's where. He'd never seen anything fly. The bumblebee wasn't around, and Superman comics weren't even invented yet. But he was so determined, he figured if he could just get his big hulk in fast forward motion, he could lift his landing gear and rest his feet for a change. And so, with his flaps-frayed-into-feathers wings, he took a tremendous running jump—and was suddenly airborne.

Look out below!

With no Civil Aeronautics regulations to tell him no-no, he could go just about anywhere he pleased. No shortage of aviation fuel, no congested airways, either. And our new, improved Proto was so naturally fierce looking, no one even tried to hijack him anyplace. He wasn't suspect either. No airport security officer had to put on white gloves and plow through the dirty laundry in his carry-on suitcase, looking for bombs and handguns.

Really, now. Can you imagine putting a couple of ironing boards on the sides of a Mack truck and expecting it to turn into a DC-3? It's the same principle as a big, floppy, heavy-boned, thick-skinned lizard taking off into the wild blue yonder. Why, if that could happen, the government ought to revamp the museum at Kitty Hawk—and make the Wright brothers move over to take second place to the first airborne lizard.

Edsel Murphy Egghead Analog:
Statistical Perfection—Five hundred goof-ups
out of five hundred tries.

Birds are carefully engineered flying machines, not lizards with lumps. However, the evolutionists don't let that bother them. They've got a good thing going, endowed professorships all over the place, fat royalty income from even fatter erudite textbooks, pretty coeds in their classes, all kinds of fringe benefits, and so they stick with it. It's too late to turn back when you've got a vested interest established.

Somehow, during the next interim of millions of years again, the flying lizard got tired of all that wing beating. The glamour of being a fly-boy faded, and he decided to settle down and raise a family. Get his feet back on the ground, you might say. So, his mind made up, he lumbered down for a beautiful five-point landing (his heavy tail was still standard flying-lizard equipment), grew a bunch of fuzz, and turned into a monkey.

The most exciting thing in the whole colossal chain of events happened when a big, hairy, reeking, itching baboon in the jungle lost his hair one night. When he got up in the morning and looked at his reflection in the swamp, he shrieked, "Good grief! I'm a people!"

And that, says the evolutionist, is where *you* came from.

To the evolutionist, it's that simple. He can actually give it all to you with a straight face. All he needs is patience and time. Given enough millions of years, anything can happen. The simple becomes the complex while he waits. Things get better by accident.

But do they really? I've never seen it happen that way. Try an experiment—with yourself as chief guinea pig.

Let yourself go for one day.

You feel like a slob.

Let yourself go for two days.

You look like a slob.

Let yourself go for three days.

You smell like a slob.

Let yourself go for four days, and you *are* a slob. And *you* don't sprout wings—other people do, trying to get away from you.

In real life, things left to themselves run down. Fast. The garden chokes up with weeds, dust gathers on the furniture, the leftovers mold in the refrigerator. In real life, things *never* get better by accident.

The theory of evolution flatly contradicts the backbone laws of science, the First and Second Laws of Thermodynamics.

These laws always show up whenever and wherever things are happening—whether they're invited or not. You just can't keep them from crashing the party. In fact, they insist on running the show, and they always get their way. Wherever the action is, these laws must always be considered.

The First Law of Thermodynamics—Thermo I—says that no one can create or destroy energy. There always is, always was, and probably always will be the same total amount of energy in the universe—exactly 100 percent—and that's all we have to work with. People usually don't worry about where it came from—they just use it. This First Law of Thermodynamics is also called the Law of Energy *Conservation*.

The Second Law of Thermodynamics, or the Energy *Transformation* law, says that *whatever* you do causes trouble. Thermo II has been called the Law of Increasing Disorder, because it acts like a typical two-year-old. It simply gets into everything, strewing it all over the place, and when you pick up the pieces, you always end up with less than you had at the

**Edsel Murphy's
Incontrovertible Laws About
Things—for Eggheads:**

1. If a thing can go wrong, it will—at the worst possible time.
2. If you play with a thing long enough, it will break. But don't worry. You can always do something with the pieces.
3. If a thing can go backward—it will. Watch out for the reversibility of inanimate objects.
4. Whenever you decide to do something first, something else always gets in the way.
5. You never need a thing—until after you've thrown it out and the garbage collector has picked it up.
6. It is always much harder to get out of a thing than to get into it.
7. Once a thing fouls up, whatever you do makes it worse. Except once in a while, when *it* makes *you* worse.
8. When a thing is self-explanatory, someone will want a ten-page report—with footnotes.

start. A contradiction of the first law? No, indeed. The portion that seems to be missing when you measure it is still around, but you can't find it. That AWOL energy is called entropy. Tired of working for a living, it has escaped to a retirement home called Unavailable Energy where it can sit incognito in a motionless rocking chair and do absolutely nothing for the rest of its days. Immediately upon retirement, it's of no further use to anyone anymore. And because everything is made of energy, and everything that happens involves a transfer of energy, and every transfer results in some unavailable energy, eventually all energy will wind up in the rest home. When it does, the rockers will be resting, too. There'll be no available energy left to keep anything in motion.

Thermo II is the reason why hot becomes cold, high becomes low, order becomes disorder, and complexity turns into randomness in every known or observed energy system left to itself with no "invisible means of support." Thermo II says that eventually everything will end up in a state of heat death, low-grade, lukewarm, icky entropy—unavailable energy. The sun *is* cooling off, and the earth *is* slowing down measurably each year, proof of this irreversible tendency of the universe to stop happening. Thermo II would have wiped out little Proto in short order—because entropy absolutely guarantees that anything less than the simplest becomes the nothingnest. Poor little Proto would have been finished off before he had a chance to develop lump number one.

Dr. Henry M. Morris, director of the Institute for Creation Research, sums it up well in the ICR Impact Series pamphlet No. 3, entitled, "Evolution, Thermodynamics, and Entropy."

The First Law is itself a strong witness against evolution, since it implies a basic condition of stability in the universe. . . .

It is the Second Law, however, that wipes out the theory of evolution. There *is* a universal process of change, and it *is* a directional change, but it is *not* an upward change. . . . Every naturally occurring transformation of energy is accompanied, somewhere, by a loss in the *availability* of energy for the future performance of work.

In this case, entropy can be expressed mathematically in terms of the total irreversible flow of heat. It expresses quantitatively the amount of energy in an energy conversion process which becomes unavailable for further work. In order for work to be done, the available energy has to "flow" from a higher level to a lower level. When it reaches the lowest level, the energy is still in existence, but no longer capable of doing work. Heat will naturally flow from a hot body to a cold body but not from a cold body to a hot body.

For this reason, no process can be 100% efficient, with all of the available energy converted into work. Some [energy] must be deployed to overcome friction and will be degraded to nonrecoverable heat energy, which will finally be radiated into space and dispersed. For the same reason, a self-contained perpetual motion machine is an impossibility.

Since, as we have noted, everything in the physical universe is energy in some form, and since in every process, some energy becomes unavailable, it is obvious that ultimately *all* energy in the universe will be unavailable energy, if present processes go on long enough. When that happens, presumably all the various forms of energy in the universe will have been gradually converted . . . into uniformly (that is, randomly) dispersed heat energy. Everything will be at the same low temperature. There will be no "differential" of energy levels, therefore no "gradient" of energy to induce its flow. No more work can be done and the universe will reach what the physicists call its ultimate "heat death."

Thus, the Second Law proves, *as certainly as science can*

prove anything whatever, that the universe had a beginning. Similarly, the First Law shows that the universe could not have begun itself. The total quantity of energy in the universe is a constant, but the quantity of *available* energy is decreasing. Therefore, as we go *backward* in time, the available energy would have been progressively greater until, finally, we would reach the beginning point, where available energy equalled total energy. Time could go back no further than this. At this point, both energy and time must have come into existence. Since energy could not create itself, the most scientific and logical conclusion to which we could possibly come is that: "In the beginning, God created the heaven and the earth."

Nice and logical, scientifically demonstrable, true. Evolutionists, however, ignore these basic laws of science and claim that with the passing of time, everything becomes better organized, more highly structured, and in better shape in an accidental sort of way. But nobody with his eyes open has ever seen it happen.

What do *you* see happening as you look around you?

Even though the theory of evolution has always been contrary to all the known, demonstrated laws of science, yet some egghead members of the scientific fraternity buy it as fact.

"Accidental happenings always produce accidental results," is a sound scientific statement. But evolution depends on accidental happenings, because that's what mutations are, unexpected, accidental changes in the design of living organisms.

**Hillism:
A Ph.D. without Jesus is a
Posthole Digger.**

On one occasion, I understand that Darwin himself got to thinking, "If my theory of evolution is true, then it came out of the head of a freak ape, because a human being is a freak ape, a mutation. But a freak ape is not capable of making a sensible decision or coming up with a learned opinion. Therefore, my own theory has to be stupid even if it's true."

That caused him some sleepless nights, I imagine. Actually, the title of one of Darwin's works hit the nail squarely on the head: *The Descent of Man,* he called it. Man has descended, all right, all the way from the superman magnificence of a Michelangelo Adam down to the sniveling sickness of the born loser of today's comic strips. But that's not the kind of "descent" Darwin had in mind. His theory of "descent" said, "Going up, please." It's a good thing Darwin wasn't an elevator operator. *Think* of the confusion!

I have presented three pagan concepts of the beginning of things, of the first man. Take your pick.

Of course, you might not like any of these concepts, preferring a history with more respectability, and ancestors more dignified than fishbait, spittoon gravy, or furry tree creatures.

In that case, there is another option open for your consideration. It's not called mythology. It's not called evolution. It's called special creation. And it says you can claim the Creator God as your Father. In his *Manufacturer's Handbook,* the Holy Bible, He tells us how some things that exist came into being. And strangely enough, all that He says there is beginning to be substantiated by scientists who are interested in the facts. (*See* Appendix II for some Bible science harmonies that will blow your mind and tune you to God's wavelength.)

But before we go into all that, let's look further at some things that exist—the visible and the invisible—that just couldn't have happened if they'd had to get here by way of the evolutionists' theories.

**Egghead's Guide for Identifying
the Scientific Disciplines:**

If it stinks—it's chemistry.
    If it hums—it's electricity.
        If it just sits there—it's physics.
            If it's green or wiggles—
                it's biology.

3

The Elephant and the Honeybee

And a Few In-Betweens That Bug the Evolutionists

My dad gave me my first lesson in creationism—the name given to the Bible account that God made everything there is—when I was about ten years old. The Barnum and Bailey circus had come to town the night before, with dozens of gaily decorated freight cars just about filling the rail yards of the town in Connecticut where I grew up.

"We're getting up before sunup tomorrow, Son," my daddy had told me the night before. "We're going to town to watch them set up the circus."

What an exciting time that was, watching my first circus go together. Those were the days before big tractors, and as I looked at all those freight cars loaded with huge tent poles, great rolls of heavy canvas, lion and tiger cages full of wild beasts, I wondered just how all that equipment could be moved, assembled, and made ready for the Big Show that evening.

While I wondered with my little boy imagination, I saw a

group of workers releasing from their cage cars an army of huge elephants, each with an iron ring around one leg, dragging a chain attached to it.

"What's the idea of turning all those elephants loose?" I asked, almost wondering if it was safe for us to be there.

"Those animals are about to do most of the work of setting up the circus," Dad explained. "Just keep your eyes open and watch what they do."

He didn't have to tell me that. I was so fascinated I kept my eyes open as wide as they would go.

Soon the giant elephants were pulling great circus wagons into place. Other elephants were carrying the huge tent poles and pegs; another group was providing the power to do all the heavy work except for driving the tent pegs into the ground. Teams of men stationed around each peg drove them rapidly into the ground with hard blows from their sledgehammers, never missing a beat.

Getting an okay from the man in charge, Dad took me closer to the elephants to show me more about them. Seeing an elephant curl his trunk around a huge tent pole weighing hundreds of pounds and place it exactly where he was directed was amazing to me.

"Now watch the end of his trunk do some delicate manipulation," Dad said, taking from his pocket a handful of peanuts.

Reaching out with that powerful trunk, which had just handled a giant tent pole, the elephant gently and delicately took the tiny peanut from Dad's hand. Grasping the nut with a small fingerlike projection attached to one side of the end of his trunk, Jumbo seemed to smile a thank-you as he opened his huge mouth and with a flip of his trunk tossed the peanut down the hatch.

I marveled at the versatility of a mechanism which could so

easily handle huge burdens and tiny yummies with such pre-cision.

A few days later, when it was time to dismantle the circus and move it to another town, I watched the elephants pulling tent stakes out of the ground. The massive wooden pegs, driven laboriously into the hard soil by sledgehammers only a few days before, were pulled out of the ground by the trunks of those elephants as effortlessly as if they had been soda straws in a milkshake at the corner drugstore.

"Let me tell you about the trunks on those elephants," Dad said as we headed home. "An elephant in captivity isn't nearly so dependent on his trunk for survival as he is in the wild state, but as you can see, it's still handy to have around. That partic-ular organ has more than twenty thousand individual muscles, all controlled by his brain not only to perform the jobs you saw him do at the circus but many more as well—uprooting giant trees in the forest, hosing the elephant down with a shower from river water, tossing an attacking tiger over his head." I suspected he had been boning up on elephants in the encyclo-pedia so he could satisfy my curiosity.

"Tame elephants are man's most valued beasts of burden in many parts of the world," Dad went on, "doing jobs that huge tractors couldn't do."

"But, Dad, how do they park all those peanut burners at night?" I asked him, my little boy mind always on the lookout for more information.

"You saw those chains attached to iron bracelets around the hind leg of each elephant?"

"Well, yes, Dad," I sputtered, "but even I can see that those chains wouldn't be nearly strong enough to hold all that power."

He nodded and explained, "You see, Son, those elephants

believe that even something as small as a piece of sash cord would restrain them because they were trained originally by being tied with huge chains. They've been conditioned to consider that any pressure at all on the hind leg means captivity."

Smart beasts? Yep, and quick learners, according to what their trainer told me as I watched them perform in one of the circus events.

But did all this learning take place over the billions of years required by evolution? Hardly. Can you imagine how useless that trunk would have been if it had popped out before the elephant knew what it might be good for? Why, it would have been in the way, just hanging there with nothing to do for millions of years. The elephant wouldn't have been able to feed himself with that awful growth on the front of his face. With evolution in charge, I suppose elephants who could afford it would have had plastic surgery—a "hose job"—to get rid of the unnecessary appendage.

As my dad wound up this lesson on how God comes up with a finished design in complete working order on the first try, he said, "Son, as you go through life and meet folks who claim that all of life just sort of happened by accident, just ask them to explain the elephant."

As the years went by, I observed many other life forms that would have died aborning if evolution had been in charge. Let's look at a few more of them.

Where I grew up in the country back in the teen years of this century, almost every farm family kept at least one beehive under the trees in its apple orchard. Partly out of necessity and partly out of just plain curiosity, I learned a lot about these sweet stingers.

Early on, I found out the best way to raid a bee tree for a rich supply of dark, sweet, wild honey. The main piece of "equipment" needed to do the job was one small boy with lots

of patience and a big appetite. When the bees were at work in
an apple tree, flower garden, or berry bush, I'd watch their
flight path and figure out the approximate location of the dead
tree where they were hiding their "loot." Then I'd look around
until I found the bee tree with a hole in the side of it and bees
going busily in and out.

The next step was to build a smoky fire at the base of the tree
to chase them away. Once stung by a mad honeybee, a boy
never forgot this step of the operation. Even so, it was a risky
venture. But bees don't like smoke and seem to feel it threatens
their city, so they all move inside and gorge themselves with
honey, filling their tanks for a quick getaway.

After the smoke treatment had made the bees vamoose, it
was time to get busy chopping down the tree with an ax or
saw—but only after arming myself with a broad-brimmed hat
covered over with mosquito netting tied around my neck under
an upturned collar, and with a pair of heavy gloves tucked
under heavy sleeves. After several painful experiences along
the way, I learned to make sure my legs were heavily covered,
too. I didn't have to read in the encyclopedia to learn that
bee stingers stay in your flesh until they are removed, and
they even seem to continue to inject poison after the bee has
flown away, leaving a vital part of himself attached to the
stinger.

Many's the time I've brushed away a stinger and made a
mudpack out of dirt mixed into a paste with boy spittle and
applied it to the bee's banqueting table—me. I'm not certain
about the actual pharmaceutical properties of that mixture, but
it helped the hurt, which was all I was really interested in.

After the tree came crashing down, it was good to have some
smoldering rags ready to stuff into the openings of the tree to
smother whatever bees might be lingering inside. "Smoking
them out," we called it. Finally, it was time to chop open the

tree and dig out the honeycomb, dripping with honey—and with pollen, dead bees, shreds of bark, bugs, ants, and a fair supply of spiders. The debris was easily filtered out by straining the honey through screenwire or cheesecloth, and to me, at least, the result was worth all the trouble it took to get it. What a gloppy feast we had! More than once, I doubled over with belly cramps from eating too much of what I had labored so hard to get.

What blessings city folks have missed!

As a boy, I marveled at the deliciousness of the food product of the honeybee, and at other things I observed about this species. One hot summer day I heard a prolonged, continuous humming sound, louder than any I had ever heard before, coming from the hive in our apple orchard. When I asked Dad about it, he said the noise was coming from the "fanner" bees, who were literally fanning hot air out of the hive so the wax wouldn't melt. Sure enough, when I held my hand to the hive, I could actually feel a hot draft leaving it.

Years later, I learned more about the mechanism of all this. On a hot day, when the temperature begins to rise, hundreds of fanning bees line up at the outlet slots of the hive, with their feet firmly anchored to the floor so they won't blow themselves away, and with both halves of their two-part wings locked together. Once situated, they begin to fan so fast as to be invisible, literally blowing the hot air out of the hive. Other workers, on the opposite side of the hive, are blowing outside air into the hive, forcing cross circulation, which cools things off. Bee air-conditioning, I call it.

To tell everything I've learned about bees over the years would take a whole book, but just look at a few mind-boggling highlights of the life of the bee that prove to me that there is no way the highly specialized honeybee could ever have evolved "by chance."

1. In cell building, the bee's body has to transform honey into wax. Because the wax cannot be shaped when it is cold, a large number of workers swarm into a mass, suspending themselves from the top of the hive, and simply hang there for up to twenty-four hours until their combined body heat brings the temperature well above 100 degrees Fahrenheit. At that point, transparent scales of wax begin to form at the abdomen slits found on each worker. When that has happened to nearly all the upside-down workers, they go into action. Each worker claws off one of her wax scales and chews it until it reaches the desired consistency, then applies it to the roof of the hive, forming a cornerstone for the structure which is to follow, composed of hexagonal tubes which will serve as storage bins, cradles, incubators, and brooders for the bee city.

2. After the wax-producing and cell-building bees have done their job, the architects come along to skillfully sculpt the structure into precisely perfect form for the use of the sixty thousand "citizens" who might occupy the city. The dimension of the corridors is just right so that two bees going in opposite directions can pass each other without colliding. Each honey storage area is tilted at an angle of 4 to 5 degrees to keep the honey from pouring out before it can thicken into place. The dimension of each individual cell is perfectly calculated so as to waste no material, and the hexagonal design is the most rigid geometric shape possible for purposes of cell design.

How do bees know all these things? Through heredity from the survival and propagation of the fittest workers? That might sound logical but worker bees are born, live, do their work, and die without ever reproducing their kind. It blows your mind, doesn't it, that man has to use calculus to determine the least material needed for a specific design, while bees do it perfectly by the instinct built into them by their Creator.

Of all living creatures, the one who gives the evolutionary

theory the blackest eye is probably the honeybee, which is far more advanced than people are in technology, social sciences, architecture, sanitation engineering, dietary technology, interpersonal relationships, group cooperation, chemical engineering, solar navigation, improvisation, and almost anything else you can name. Living in cities or colonies of up to ninety thousand population, they operate in a cooperative way unknown among any other creatures. With no police departments, no jails, no strikes, no slowdowns, no labor shortages, no divorces, no gossips, no backbiters, no murders, no drunken drivers, no political divisions or elections, no greed or crooked citizens, their level of civilization is far above any other I've ever heard about. Does their level of success have anything to do with the fact that a queen bee rules the roost and that women do all the work except for the task of fertilizing the eggs of the queen? Who can say? All I know is that their system is so complicated, the odds against even a tiny part of it happening by chance are more than astronomical.

Glass-walled hives have been built so the habits of the bee could be carefully studied, and what has been learned about them is incredible—but completely true. Let's look at it a little more before we move on.

During its short life of a few weeks, each worker bee takes turns at performing every task—without apparent supervision or need for a management manual to maintain incentive or boost worker morale.

The first job performed by the worker is that of sanitation engineering. She cleans out the brood cells and makes them ready to receive new eggs from the queen. After three days on the janitorial detail, she graduates to the position of nursemaid and feeds pollen and honey to the wormlike grubs, or larvae, hatched from the queen's eggs. From the sixth to the twelfth day, she feeds the larvae and the queen on a special diet of royal jelly, which she secretes from her own head. From day twelve to day sixteen, the worker bee practices a career as architect builder of wax cells. From about day seventeen through day nineteen, she is a receiving clerk, unloading nectar and pollen brought to the hive by the foragers you see working in your flower garden. Around the twentieth day, she takes over as security guard at the entrance of the hive, looking out for intruders or other threats to the well-being of the colony. Beginning at the third week and continuing for the rest of her life, she is a forager, collecting and delivering nectar and pollen.

"Whew!" you say? No wonder we have the expression, "Busy as a bee."

Meanwhile, this schedule is not a rigid one but can be readily adapted to meet special needs. In one experiment, a bee researcher rid the hive of all except forager bees. Although they were well past nursing age, these older bees immediately grew new nursing glands and began feeding the babies again. When a hive was left without foraging bees, the babies began to take over the foraging job in just a few days.

Who programs each bee so she knows exactly what jobs need doing and who is to do them? Research has revealed that every worker bee goes through a daily inspection routine for herself, spending about a third of her time in careful inspection of cells, larvae, food supplies, hive, and sanitary conditions as well as nursery needs. What she observes is cranked into her schedule for the day in order the meet the needs of the community.

One of the means by which the bees communicate with one another is by dancing. Certain kinds of dances tell the location and condition of nectar to be harvested for the food supply. Dances convey the number of workers needed to do a particular job. If something happens to the queen bee, there is a plan for developing and choosing a new one. A colony knows when it ought to divide in two, for optimum conditions for bee living.

How's your belief in evolution holding up? Is it still alive? There are a few diehards in every crowd, so let's look at a few more examples of things that couldn't happen if evolution had to do it.

Take the case of the sea slugs that shoot poison spears. Living in shallow waters along coastlines, these slugs feed primarily on the deadly sea anemones. The anemones look like beautiful flowers, but are sinister danger in alluring disguise, armed with thousands of stinging spears on their tentacles. At the slightest touch, the tentacles shoot poison stingers into fish or other intruders, paralyzing them and drawing them into the anemone's stomach to be digested.

How is it that sea slugs can feed on them without being stung to death in the process? Evolution? Or God's design?

This amazing mystery of nature is possible because the sea slug is equipped with pouches on its outer surface insulated with moving hairs that sweep the stinging cells into its stomach where they are stored in an arsenal. When a hungry fish tries to take a bite of the sea slug, the poor fish gets stung in the mouth by the stinging cells that the treacherous anemone manufactured for its own defense!

Can you imagine the infinitely complex series of "coincidences" that would be required for the blind forces of evolution to produce this relationship? The sea slug would have had to evolve some weapon to keep the stinging cells from exploding at the slightest touch. And it would have had to evolve a selective digestive system that does not digest stinging cells but does digest the edible parts of the anemone. The sea slug would be faced with the necessity of evolving pouches and tubes with moving hairs as well as a system by which it could store the stinging cells in an orderly fashion ready to be fired at a moment's notice.

If I were an evolutionist, I wouldn't try to figure out how all this could happen. I'd throw up my hands, relinquish my vain and foolish philosophy, and say, "Let God be God."

Still some foot draggers? That's okay. Honest doubters are worth persuading. Because they don't come to faith lightly, once they're there, they stick tight. So here are a few more persuaders for you.

Look at the navigational system of birds. How could evolution ever explain how the common pigeon switches from one navigational system in sunny weather to a totally different one when the skies are cloudy and gray? How could an evolutionist account for the magnetic compass mechanism inside its head? And what about the warbler that spends its summers in Europe, raises its young, and takes off for deepest Africa, leaving the kids behind in the nest until they can qualify as long-distance fliers? A few weeks later, without the benefit of charts or flight data or previous experience, the young birds head for Africa to rejoin Mom and Pop. Pretty neat trick, wouldn't you say? How do they do it? Real scientists have proven that these birds navigate by stellar navigation, the same unfailingly accurate system used today by our astronauts, one that never wanders off course as do our best mechanical computer-controlled airliner control mechanisms.

Where does the know-how come from—the random, accidental happenings of evolutionists' theories, or something put in them by a Creator God from the beginning of time, so that when they emerge from the egg, they are fully programmed for all they will be required to do to fulfill their own unique life cycle?

Let's look at another far-out example, this one in the bug

world, showing what a bug-turned-chemist can do when he decides the enemy needs clobbering. The millipede—*apheloria corrugata,* if you want to get technical—is highly skilled in organic chemistry and uses his great wisdom, which he acquired without having to pay tuition at some great university somewhere, to ward off enemy attacks, much as men do with chemical warfare. Each side of his body is equipped with glands that produce the liquid compound mandelonitrile. In another part of its chemical laboratory, it carries a catalyst, which when mixed with the other stuff causes it to break down into benzaldehyde plus hydrogen cyanide—a real killer.

This little creature, having done his chemical thing, just rests on his many legs and watches his enemies flee in all directions while he isn't affected at all by the death vapors he has just manufactured. How come? We don't know—unless an all-knowing Creator designed it to work just like that for His own purposes.

And how about the archerfish? If you ever find an apparent or sensible reason—except a Creator's sense of humor—for this little weirdo's existence, let me know. The archerfish goes swimming along on a bug-hunting expedition. Suddenly he spies an overhanging branch close to the water. Almost holding his breath, he waits quietly below it for a fly or other insect to alight. When it does, the archerfish squirts a single drop of water so forcefully and with such deadly precision at his target, that it is blasted from the branch and tumbles into the water where the archerfish slurps him up for lunch and swims happily away. What kind of evolution would it take to explain a habit pattern like that? Or does the Creator simply enjoy variety?

Ever hear of sonar, a method of navigation in which sound waves are bounced off shorelines to indicate distances? Bats have used it ever since bats began, long before we got smart enough to apply the system for locating underwater enemy submarines. Sonar is similar to radar, using sound waves instead of radar's electrical waves. The sound wave is generated and bounced off whatever surface happens to be in the way, coming back as a reflected signal after a time interval proportionate to the distance from the subject.

How does the little bug-hunting bat utilize this complex principle that took our best brains so long to catch on to? As the bat goes out on his nightly foray for bugs in the dark, he sends out a series of high-pitched chirps, mostly in a frequency inaudible to human ears. Each chirp lasts only about two milliseconds, and beginning at a frequency of about 100,000 cycles per second, diminishes to half that frequency. The spectrum of frequencies acts as a sorting mechanism to enable the bat to distinguish between larger and smaller objects. The shorter wavelengths are reflected back from smaller objects, enabling the bat to capture only insects of proportions suitable for his appetite.

How could evolution ever think up a plan like that?

Whales, dolphins, and porpoises use a similar system to navigate with exact precision in underwater darkness. In fact, our best scientific brains have failed to duplicate the marvelously developed sonar mechanisms of these denizens of the deep.

And have you ever wondered how accidental happenings could result in that highly skilled artisan, the web-spinning spider? I have. Here's a creature that converts what he eats into where he lives, traps his food, and rests from his labors.

It's hard for me to imagine the complex process in which several types of protein are manufactured in such a tiny mechanism, producing the numerous types of filaments of thread and weaving them into intricate patterns without a single blueprint or instruction manual. I mean, spiders have to be born smart.

If you have ever visited a factory where nylon thread is manufactured, you will have some slight idea of the complexity of such a process.

First the raw material, or cellulose, is stripped from cotton bolls or other organic sources, after which it is completely digested until it becomes a thick and gloppy chemical soup containing microscopically small particles of debris. To rid the soup of the debris—which must be totally eliminated so that it cannot clog the tiny holes in the spinnerets through which the soup will be squeezed to form the thread—the liquid nylon is forced through gigantic filter presses made of extremely fine filtering material several feet in thickness. Enormous pressures have to be exerted in order to force the material through the presses.

Even with the most careful handling, sometimes a tiny particle gets through and plugs the holes in the spinnerets, calling a halt to the whole operation. Furthermore, the sensitivity of the material to humidity and other weather factors means that the factory must be carefully air-conditioned. Even then, static electricity often causes the extruding filaments to tangle and upset the manufacturing process. I have watched this process as miles and miles of nylon thread were being produced under the best conditions man could devise and suddenly something would set in and snafu the whole operation. And yet the tiny spider does it all perfectly within a body weighing only a tiny fraction of an ounce.

Have you ever watched a spider at work? I have. And I have never ceased to marvel at the great engineering skills programmed into them. Has the spider been programmed by the random, accidental happenings of evolution, or by a Creator God of infinite wisdom?

In all my observation of spider engineering, I have failed to discover any gigantic filter presses for removing foreign materials from the liquid thread. I have never seen a spider shut down his factory to take time out to clean out the microscopic holes in his spinnerets.

Quite aside from the manufacturing process, look at what he does with the thread he produces. Just how does he know that every strand serves an engineering purpose in lending strength and endurance to the web that must be able to weather all sorts of abuse—changes in humidity, rainstorms, wind, struggling trapped insects, and the like? There's no such thing as air-conditioning where he works, and no about-to-be-trapped insect handles the delicate web with care, either.

Have you ever wondered how a spider keeps from getting trapped in his own sticky web? I have. From my own experiences with running into scary, sticky, spider webs in the woods when I was a boy, I know there has to be a real trick to that.

There is one especially fascinating spider skilled in the engineering art of lifting great weights over long distances. When he kills at ground level an insect too big to eat on the spot but big enough to put in his deep freeze so he'll have food for weeks to come, he needs to elevate the dead body to web level, which might be several feet above the ground in a bush. Impossible? With evolution, yes, but with an intelligent Creator behind him, just watch him go.

First he attaches a strand of new-spun thread to the dead body, having already attached the other end of the thread to the twig where he has built his nest. The spider just happens to know that as it dries, the web filament will shrink, raising his prey a microscopic distance from the earth. The next strand will be a little shorter than the first one, because the carcass is already closer to the meat storage area of the spider's home. Each shrinking strand does its part in raising the huge bug burger a little closer to home. How does the tiny spider know that after hundreds or even thousands of cycles the burger will rest safely in the center of its web?

According to the latest reports I've heard, evolution hasn't ever found any fossil evidence that spiders have evolved, leaving no sensible answer other than that of special creation by an exceedingly special Creator.

Have you ever thought about spiders and how they operate as a powerful rebuttal to the claims of evolutionists? I have, and one day I asked one of them, "How does a spider know how to spin a web?"

"By instinct," he murmured, shrugging his shoulders. So far, so good, but there was more to our conversation.

"What is instinct?" I asked him in a friendly manner.

"Er—ah—inherited memory." That, too, was a very logical reply.

He could even tell me from whom the spider inherited his knowledge and wisdom. "From his parents, of course," he explained patiently. But when we worked our way back to where the first spider in the world got his knowledge of all these things, we had run out of the possibility of inherited wisdom as the source of spider wisdom. There wasn't any great great grandpa to hand down anything to the first generation.

"Where did the original spider inherit *his* memory to pass on to the next generation?" I might have asked then. It's the kind of question that will get immediate results. The evolutionist will be moved to consult his wristwatch and remember that he's about to be late for an extremely urgent appointment somewhere. Anywhere will do.

But let me tell you about another of these remarkable little engineers. There's a certain little spider, not much bigger than the button on a man's shirt, who lives on the North Pacific Coast. She makes her nest in the empty shell of a clam or other bivalve, sometimes in a gigantic abalone shell. But she doesn't build her nest in the shell when it is lying on the ground. Someone might come along and step on her babies. She needs to lift the shell up in the bough of a low shrub where it can be hidden in comparative safety.

Now, the tiny spider weighs barely a fraction of an ounce and the shell may weigh half a pound. How can she do it? Does she have to call in the neighbors for a barn raising? No, she's fully equipped and programmed to do it all by herself, using the same techniques as the first spider did to get fresh meat up to her dining room: spin and wait for shrinking, spin and wait for shrinking, enough times to get the job done. Night and day she labors until the shell gradually swings into position up in the bough of the bush. Then she spins strong cables to hold the site of her future home in place, lining the shell with silken threads and spinning a waterproof roof over it with a tiny door to the outside.

At last she is ready to go inside, settle down, lay her eggs, and rear her brood in peace and safety.

Could evolution account for the intricacy of any of that? Or is the only reasonable explanation that there is a Creator who has imparted to every creature the wisdom it needs to survive in a hostile environment?

Another living creature full of embarrassment for evolutionists is the ouzel bird, sometimes called the water ouzel or the dipper. This squatty, silky, perky little black bird, always busily on the move, by its very existence casts a cloud of divine ridicule over the theory of evolution.

I first noticed this strange little contraption while fishing on a lake in northern Wisconsin. It was a beautiful October day, with hardly a breeze blowing and not a fish biting. As I lazily cast my muskie plug toward the shore from our drifting boat, I noticed a pair of what appeared to be miniature black ducks busily chasing flies several hundred feet from our boat. Looking more closely, I saw that their behavior was not like any duck I knew about. They darted about and at times seemed to be actually running on the surface of the water. As I watched, they suddenly dropped straight down, as though an unseen hand had yanked them straight to the bottom.

I had often seen ducks dive to the lake bottom for food, but they always did it by upending themselves and paddling their way down. But these little birds didn't dive—they simply sank straight down like a submarine. After several minutes of waiting, I still hadn't seen them surface. I nudged my fishing buddy who was half-asleep in the stern.

"Hey, Jim! Wake up! I have something to ask you."

Yawning and rubbing his eyes, he shook himself awake.

"What's your problem, Hill?"

"I'm not sure. Maybe I dreamed it, but a few minutes ago I saw a pair of black birds chasing bugs. While I was watching, they sank like rocks and haven't come up yet. That's much too long for any bird to stay under water," I sputtered.

"Hold it, Hill," Jim laughed. "Nothing to be alarmed about. What you probably saw was a pair of ouzel birds, which are often seen in this part of the country."

"Ouzel bird? Never heard of it. How come it can stay under water forever?"

"Well, it can't, exactly. And it doesn't. Just looks like it to the unpracticed eye." He went on to tell me how the ouzel bird can operate exactly like a submarine, pumping water into or out of its storage tanks so it can ride high on the water, partially submerged, or drop out of sight. Once on the bottom, it can walk along, getting its fill of the smorgasbord goodies on the lake bottom. Then suddenly he'll run to the shore, wade up the bank, shake himself dry, swallow his food, and start all over again.

"But why didn't I *see* him come up?" I asked, not quite satisfied with his explanation.

"You just didn't look in the right place, Hill." Jim shrugged matter-of-factly. "You see, the ouzel never does the expected thing. Just watch, and I'll show you." With that, Jim started the outboard motor and headed for the pair of ouzels which had appeared again on top of the water not far from our drifting boat. Instead of panicking and taking off in a direction away from us, as ducks usually do, that pair simply sank straight down out of sight again a few yards ahead of us.

"Now watch carefully, or you'll miss them," Jim warned.

They traveled under water, faster than I would have thought possible, and suddenly bobbed up way off to our left, scooting after bugs on the surface again.

That day I learned that ouzels are actually friends of the fisherman, because they feed on insects and snails detrimental to fish propagation.

Can you imagine evolution producing the ouzel, whose main purpose in life seems to be to protect fish eggs? I can't.

Now let's look at an example of cooperation between the plant and animal world, and then we'll be ready to move on to a look at how it really happened.

Our subject now is the yucca plant, which appears in abundance in desert areas, where it produces rapier sharp leaves and fragrant, beautiful white blossoms.

I first learned about this unusual plant when my friend Bob stopped his car along a dusty roadside one day. We were on our way to a meeting and had plenty of time to spare.

"Hill," he said, "you're always interested in the odd and unusual. Take a look at this yucca and let me tell you about its strange life-style."

Walking a few yards off the highway, he pointed to a cactus-like plant and said, "Those blossom-buds indicate that a special event is about to take place. Hold on a minute. Maybe I can show you how it works."

Bob knelt in the sand and scratched around at the base of the plant until he unearthed a cocoon. "Here's what we're looking for," he said, "the pronuba moth just about ready to come out of its cocoon and do its job—pollinating the blossoms that are about to open."

"What's so unusual about that?" I wondered. This is what he told me.

On certain nights of the year, which just happen to be the nights when the yucca blossoms open fully, the yucca moth emerges from its cocoon at the base of the plant. Attracted by the blossom's powerful aroma, which doesn't attract other pollinating insects, the moth gathers a large load of pollen, shapes it into a ball, and flies to a blossom on an entirely different yucca plant. Here, with her egg-laying spiked tail, she drills a hole in the pistil (or stigma) of the flower, and deposits her eggs among the seed cells there. Then she stuffs the pollen load down the hole, mashing it down to reach the seed cells where she just deposited her eggs.

This "night out" is the only one the tiny white yucca moth will ever enjoy. Having done her thing with those two blossoms, she promptly dies, never seeing the fruits of her labors and not acquiring the information that there will ever be any fruit. Ruled by instinct programmed into her, the moth simply contributes to an amazing life cycle which is only just beginning as she takes off for moth heaven.

The desert heat incubates the moth eggs and ripens the yucca seeds, all at a predetermined rate so that when the larvae hatch out, they will be surrounded by abundant food. The baby moths, in caterpillar form, consume their share of the seeds, leaving plenty for the next cycle. Then they chop a hole through the bottom of the seed pod, spin an "escape cable," on which they slide down to the sand at the base of the yucca plant, burrow their way into the sand, spin a cocoon around themselves, and wait for the next life cycle to begin when the next open-blossom fragrance fills the air of another hot desert night.

How could evolution account for the arrival of both the plant and the moth, each dependent on the other for survival, with built-in knowledge of how to go about carrying out their complex responsibilities? Just one error in judgment, such as the moth's visiting two blossoms on the same plant, would upset the entire process. Cross-pollination between the separate plants is vital to life for moth and plant alike.

How does the blossom know to open for its one-night stand on the very night when the moth is emerging from its cocoon for its one winged venture into the air?

The Creator must have had a good laugh as He came up with this one, challenging evolutionists, "Let's see you explain this one." But the evolutionists haven't yet admitted their defeat.

In a science seminar where I was speaking one day, an evolutionist came up with this question: "But, Hill, don't you think that we could have gotten here by way of the mitosis route—where the original single cell continued to split over the eons of time, eventually producing the human race through the process of evolution?"

"Nope," I told him, sure of my ground because I had read the *Manufacturer's Handbook* about how the Creator made everything all by Himself.

"Just what do you find wrong with that theory?" he asked me.

"Tell me exactly how that could happen," I challenged him, believing that if he really thought it through, he'd discover for himself that the theory is leakier than a worn-out sieve.

"Well," he stopped to clear his throat importantly, "let's assume that each generation produced a little more 'acquired behavior' for the benefit of future generations and that beneficial mutations contributed to the overall picture so that over the billions of years—well, here we are!"

He was grinning when he stopped for breath, but his smile faded as we discussed details of such a scheme, including such unanswerable questions as: "Has there ever been a 'good' mutation?" and "Who said that acquired behavior patterns and knowledge can be passed on genetically?" and "Where did sex enter the picture?" He had to acknowledge that it is a proven scientific fact that mutations are not beneficial, and that learned behavior and acquired knowledge cannot be passed down genetically from one generation to another but must be gained by each succeeding group of offspring. Instinct, on the other hand, could be programmed into each species by a Creator who designed the system so creatures wouldn't have to learn things by trial and error, wasting time with a lot of wrong things as humans often do. Another difficulty he acknowledged was that once a single little Proto evolved into something higher, it would have to look forever to find a monkey mate that had evolved in the same direction.

The evolutionist had to admit too that there is no his and hers among protozoans or other single-celled creatures. They're totally sexless and therefore incapable of transmitting love-making tendencies to their offspring. Self-pollination in no way parallels the complex process of procreation through the male and female types. At what point in the cell-splitting process did this sudden creative ability appear?

Our conversation ended that day without his having decided anything conclusive, but I believe he was a little more open to consider what really happened. How about you? Are you ready now to hear what the Creator has to say about all this?

To whet your appetite a little, you might like to read what God thinks about the evolutionists' denial of Himself as the Creator of all things:

> Now the holy anger of God is disclosed from Heaven against the godlessness and evil of those men who render truth dumb and impotent by their wickedness. It is not that they don't know the truth about God; indeed he has made it quite plain to them. For since the beginning of the world the invisible attributes of God, e.g., his eternal power and deity, have been plainly discernible through things which he has made and which are commonly seen and known, thus leaving men without a rag of excuse. They knew all the time that there is a God, yet they refused to acknowledge him as such, or to thank him for what he is or does. Thus they became fatuous in their argumentations, and plunged their silly minds still further into the dark. Behind a façade of "wisdom" they became just fools, fools who would exchange the glory of the immortal God for an image of a mortal man, or of creatures that run or fly or crawl. They gave up God. . . .
>
> Romans 1:18–24 PHILLIPS

Quite a statement about egghead intelligence, isn't it? As for me, I'd rather have the mind of Christ.

And now, on with the Creator's account of how these things *really* happened.

4

How Did It Really Happen?

What God Says About It

According to the first chapter of the *Manufacturer's Handbook,* the Holy Bible, "In the beginning, God created the heaven and the earth" (Genesis 1:1). He doesn't just tell us *that* He did it, He tells us *how* He did it. He describes the raw materials and the scientific processes by which He converted what was there in the beginning of time into what we know exists today.

In the beginning, "the earth was without form, and void," God says, "and darkness was upon the face of the deep" (Genesis 1:2).

Prior to its transformation into matter, everything was just raw energy. It was without form and void, that is, it was invisible and empty.

Way back when I took college physics, we were taught that there was no way to transform energy into matter. "Can't be done," the eggheads told us. They also claimed the atom was the smallest particle in existence and not subject to reduction. Have we ever learned a lot since then!

It's a good thing God didn't attend the same college I did. He'd have been taught that He couldn't have created the world out of the raw materials available to Him because energy couldn't be transformed into matter, according to early twentieth-century scientists. If I had been reading—and believing—the Bible in those days, I could have saved my tuition money and had all the right answers instead of the wrong ones.

All of creation was made from something invisible—energy. God says it right there in Genesis and also in the New Testament, in Hebrews 11:3 (TLB): "By faith—by believing God—we know that the world and the stars—in fact, all things—were made at God's command; and that they were all made from things that can't be seen." Pretty good hint at the atomic theory of matter, isn't it? But men were a long time coming to understand the truth. They chose to believe their own imaginings—until the facts clobbered them over the head with the revealed truth of God.

The Bible had said for a long time that man's wisdom is foolishness to God, but my professors didn't believe that. They said, "God's wisdom is foolishness to us—we don't understand what He is saying—so we'll make up some wisdom of our own." They fed me a lot of their "wisdom," and it's taken a long time for me to get it all out of my system. Textbooks and encyclopedias are still full of it.

When Albert Einstein came along with his amazing discovery of the relationship between energy and matter, he was in direct agreement with the account of creation in the first part of Genesis. Relativity had been there from the very beginning, before mankind got around to inventing science and mathematics.

At first, when Einstein said, "$E = mc^2$" (energy = mass times the speed of light squared), nobody believed him. Scientists shook their heads and said, "Well, the fellow's sort of soft in the head—roof trouble, you know. He says you can transform energy into matter at the speed of light, but we know better. Energy can't be transformed into matter. No way. It's never been done, therefore it's not possible. That's all there is to it." They closed the case—temporarily.

As things went on, however, and scientists began to learn more and more about how things *really* worked, lo and behold, they found themselves scratching their heads and saying, "You know, I believe Albert has something there. Matter of fact, from what we've been seeing in the laboratory, what he says has got to be true!"

I can just imagine God chuckling when they finally caught on. He had known it all along, from before the day when His Spirit moved and He spoke to the chaos of energy that was without form and void and said, "Let there be light." And at His Word, there was light. Energy at the speed of light—186,000 miles per second—is transformable into matter, and so the visible world came into being.

After Einstein came along, some men began to see what God was talking about.

[Did you ever stop to think about the fact that there was light (Genesis 1:3) before the creation of the sun (Genesis 1:14–18)? That light was Jesus.[1] He claimed to be the Light of the world, and He was with God from the beginning (John 1:1–3). Nothing was made without Him. And if you read the next to the last chapter of the *Manufacturer's Handbook,* you'll see that in the New Jerusalem, Jesus, the Lamb of God, will again be the exclusive Light of the world, just as He was before the sun and moon: "And the city had no need of the sun, neither of the moon, to shine in it: for the glory of God did lighten it, and the Lamb is the light thereof" (Revelation 21:23).]

The world of science has for some time sought for an overall concept or unified field theory which would integrate all systems into a single neat mathematical formula. Such a formula would enable us to crank a few numbers into a computer to give us simple answers to all things scientific. Einstein's theory of relativity was a step in this direction, but further research has revealed more unknowns.

I believe the perfect unified field theory or coordinated continuum of all systems is contained in the "God said, Let there be light" statement in Genesis 1:3. At that moment, there came into existence not only the visible light which we detect when it bounces off things, but the entire spectrum of wavelengths from the highest to the lowest frequency patterns, including all the forces needed to make the whole creation operational—mechanical forces (such as gravity), electrical forces, magnetic forces, nuclear forces, atomic forces, and whatever other forces there might be that we don't even know about yet.

When God created all that is, He didn't attach a label that said "Batteries Not Included." Everything He made was checked out with the Manufacturer's guarantee that it was good. And not only was everything guaranteed to work, everything was—and still is—guaranteed to work *together* for good with the other elements of His creation, even when we goof it. I've never heard a guarantee like that from any other manufacturer, have you? They always leave themselves an escape hatch or two where they can weasel out of their promises. But God stands behind His product forever. With Him, perfection is the order of the day.

In modern terminology, you might say that the universe is

God's master computer, and that the Bible, or *Manufacturer's Handbook,* as I like to call it, is an encyclopedic program manual telling us how to make the computer work for best results in our lives in the here and the hereafter. The seven-letter analog, "God said," is like a command in a computer software program. Properly used—without the slightest deviation from the programmer's instructions—a command for an ordinary personal computer will accomplish the exact purpose for which the command was designed. Change the command in any way, and you won't get what you're after. Instead, you may get some kind of ERROR message—maybe even flashing red lights or a Bronx cheer, depending on the programming built into your computer.

Operators of ordinary personal and business computers know that for best results, they must always follow the instructions exactly. That's how it is for King's kids operating God's master computer too. Following instructions exactly guarantees best results. Doing your own thing guarantees trouble. What are His instructions? The *Manufacturer's Handbook* is full of them. Do any of these "God saids" sound familiar to you?

Abide in Me. . . . Be anxious for nothing. . . . Call upon the name of the Lord. . . . Do unto others as you would have them do unto you. . . . Earnestly desire the best gifts. . . . Forgive, that your heavenly Father may forgive you. . . . Give and it will be given unto you. . . . Hear the Word of the Lord. . . . Incline your heart to the Lord. . . . Judge not that ye be not judged. . . . Keep His commandments. . . . Love your enemies. . . .

(For information about a whole book full of *ABCs for King's Kids,* send a stamped, self-addressed envelope to *Star Books, 408 Pearson Street, Wilson, NC 27893.)

Believe it or not, every instruction in the *Manufacturer's Handbook*—and there are thousands of them—is perfectly designed to produce results. Because God is constantly in control of all particles, wave forms, frequencies, and wavelengths, it is no great thing for Him to issue a "God said" code word that can change things from glory to glory right before our eyes.

When Jesus said, "Peace, be still" (*see* Mark 4:39), the storm had to calm down. The simple code words, "Lazarus, come forth" (*see* John 11:43), opened the grave, instilled new life into a corpse, and provided the locomotion necessary for obedience to that command—even with bound-up hands and feet!

No wonder Jesus said, ". . . Man does not live on bread alone, but on every word that comes from the mouth of God" (Matthew 4:4 NIV). It is God's Word that made the universe and His Word that keeps it spinning. When God's own creative code words begin to abide in our hearts and come from our mouths, we're going to see things that up to now we have only dreamed of. All of God's words are eternal, speed-of-light words, accomplishing the purposes for which He sends them. And Jesus told us that we could do the things He did—and greater things (*see* John 14:12).

Because God is God, we shouldn't be surprised at the thought that someday we'll be able to swap time for space and go from here to there with no time lapse. For now, science has to call such things aberrations or anomalies, as if they were something out of the ordinary, but God seems to be saying, "That's simply how I work when you take Me at My Word." In King James English, it comes out like this:

. . . Eye hath not seen, nor ear heard, neither have entered into the heart of man, the things which God hath prepared for them that love him.

1 Corinthians 2:9

I'm getting ready to find out about some of those mysteries, aren't you? Meanwhile, all these things are understandably a little hard for our finite minds to completely grasp. But at least we know He tells us to praise Him, and that He inhabits the praises of His people, so until we get better understanding, we can go with what we've got.

Meanwhile, Liz Rogers, my partner in the King's Kids' Korner, and I have been compiling from the *Manufacturer's Handbook* some King's Kids' Kartridges to Konfess—for all different purposes. We have Kartridges for healing, for looking for a mate, for finding a job, for getting out of debt, and for solving almost any other problem you might have. Each Kartridge is composed entirely of the Word of God, helping you to pray the Word of God in your situation and watch the answer come forth. (A self-addressed, stamped envelope will get you further details: King's Kids' Korner, Box 8655, Baltimore, MD 21240.)

But we were talking about making matter out of energy, weren't we, before I got sidetracked into computers.

On Long Island, at Brookhaven National Laboratories, there is a tremendous piece of equipment into which we can introduce electromagnetic energy by dropping in a piece of matter, a proton, whirling it around at a tremendous rate just under the speed of light and dropping another proton in its path. The energy of the first one, plus the impact of the second upon it, produces a third one. Matter out of energy. This has been demonstrated and photographed and checked out thoroughly.[2]

In addition to creating matter from energy, we can change shoe leather—or any other material—into gold. In the old days, alchemists tried to change base metals into gold—and failed. Because such gold costs about half a million dollars an ounce, we don't have a very long waiting list for it, but if you've got the curiosity and the money to back it up, we can do it for you.

Today the world of science knows how to transform atomic structures. And it has advanced to the state where we can transform energy into matter, though once we were taught that not even God could do that.

In the beginning, when the Spirit of God moved (Genesis 1:2), He interfaced two gases—hydrogen and oxygen—and water appeared—H_2O. As soon as there was motion, an atom of oxygen and two atoms of hydrogen were joined in a wedding ceremony, and they became one. Water was the first molecule in creation.

Water is the backbone of life, the basic building block of man. All of us are all wet—90 percent water.

Water is one of the most mysterious molecules we know anything about. The H_2O molecule is subject to practically no tampering. Hydrogen and oxygen appear in exclusive combination in only two forms—water (H_2O), or hydrogen peroxide (H_2O_2). Beyond that, God says, "Don't fool around, because water is basic to life."

We can take carbon and hydrogen and produce trillions of combinations—no computer yet has figured out exactly how many—but H_2O and H_2O_2 have an exclusive on their joining. No other combination can get a franchise.[3]

Water behaves contrary to some laws observable in the behavior of other substances. Water, as you know, is made up of a pair of gases. Ordinarily, if you heat gases, they expand; if you cool them, they contract. Most of the other gases behave like you expect them to. But water has an independent streak. When you heat water, it expands, but when you cool it, it contracts only up to a certain point, and then it begins to expand again. If it didn't, every body of water would freeze from the bottom up, and in a few hours, all the marine life—the algae and everything else—would freeze to death.

Edsel Murphy Egghead Analog: Indeterminacy—The odds against a thing working without a hitch three times in a row.

A full 70 percent of our oxygen supply comes from algae in the water, so God's special arrangement for the contraction and expansion of H_2O is vital for us. It's as if He said, "Water, you must begin to expand again before you freeze solid and fall to the bottom of the pond."

God always works out special arrangements where they're needed. If He didn't, we wouldn't be here thinking about it.

There's something else highly interesting about this water business. In Genesis 1, God says He divided the water into two groups, the waters above the sky and the waters below the sky (Genesis 1:6–8). He didn't only divide the water into two locations, He divided it into two forms, the liquid form with which the oceans are filled and vast amounts in dry storage in powdered form to be used in replenishing our supply through the springs in the sea and the rocks of the earth.

Eyebrows are shooting up all over the place, and I hear someone squawking, "Hold on a minute, Hill. I've never heard of such a thing as powdered water!"

Well, you have now, and if you want to hear more about it, read on.

But first, let's learn something else about the liquid variety. How can you join atoms of two gases—oxygen and hydrogen—together to make a drinkable molecule? Just burn hydrogen gas in the presence of free oxygen and water will come forth. You can try it for yourself. The next time you come across a cylinder of hydrogen gas with a suitable burner nozzle, simply ignite the gas, hold a piece of cold metal close to the flame, and water will immediately begin dripping from the metal.

And there's an even simpler way to observe this. Next time you see a car being started on a cold morning, notice the cloud coming out the exhaust pipe. Among other things, that is water vapor. If the weather is extremely cold, so the pipe does not heat quickly, after a few seconds you will see water beginning to trickle out of the end of the pipe.

Where does all that water come from? It is being manufactured inside the engine as hydrogen atoms, contained in the hydrocarbon fuel, are burned in the presence of free oxygen sucked into the engine through the intake valves on the downward stroke of the pistons. And it's not just a small amount of water. For every gallon of fuel burned, a large percentage of that gallon comes forth in the form of water vapor. That's one reason why internal combustion engines are so inefficient. The average automobile engine converts only about 25 percent of the fuel into go power. Some of the rest of it is used up as power to manufacture water. If you keep your eyes open, you'll see many other instances in which hydrogen unites with oxygen in the presence of fire to build water molecules.

To me, the God who set such laws in motion way back at the beginning is far more impressive than the "no-god" of evolution who just sits around and waits for something good to happen by accident. Water, being the backbone of all living things—the basic building block of all creation—must of necessity be easily produced, and our great Creator God has so arranged it.

The next time someone tells you you're all wet, don't take it as an insult—take it as an only slightly exaggerated statement of a scientific truth. What would be left of you if all the water were removed would be only about two dollars' worth of fertilizer, even at today's inflated prices.

Ready now to hear about the powdered variety of water?

Everywhere you turn these days, you can hear someone carping about the pollution of our water supply.

"There's no such thing as pure water anymore," I read in one ad for water conditioners. "All of our water supply has become polluted, and you need our little Dandy-Andy filter for safe drinking."

Offhand, the average person might be inclined to fall for the pitch. And it's true that on planet earth it is impossible to find a lake, stream, ocean, or well that has not received some degree of contamination. The water you drank after you brushed your teeth might have come to you through the interior plumbing system of six camels, a couple of donkeys, and a baboon or two. The next drink you take might have started out as Cleopatra's bath water.

All of which is a roundabout way of acknowledging that there's a pretty good possibility that all free-flowing water on planet earth has been used for thirst quenching, Laundromatting, spot removing, fire fighting, lawn sprinkling, cooking, bathing, and the like many times before it got to you or me. If you didn't know any better, you might even wind up agreeing with the atheist who griped, "If there is a Creator God, He certainly goofed it when he failed to protect the human race against ruining its water supply. He should have designed a water source totally free of any possibility of contamination from people and animals."

The fact is that in the very beginning God did design for us a source of water in pure, unadulterated, unpolluted form, and stored it on planet earth in powdered, dry-packed form. This "virgin water" is nonflowing, dry, and unusable until it is "cooked out" of its storage capsule by high temperatures. You might call it water in "unassembled" form, and it is being continuously turned loose by God's perfect supply system. The Bible refers to "springs of the sea" (Job 38:16).

On the ocean bottom in many parts of the world, this fresh, unused, virgin water is bubbling up at the rate of billions of gallons a day, being released from its dry-storage state into liquid form by the heat of underground volcanic action. By heating the rocks which contain this dry-form water, God liberates it so that it can come to us in a pure state and thus replenish our old, used supply.

A person can live a long time without taking food into his body, but even a few days without water can be fatal. With water being absolutely indispensable to our ability to stay alive, you would really expect God to be way out ahead of our best efforts to ruin our water supply, wouldn't you? And so He is. In His infinite wisdom, He has done some amazing things to provide pure water for His people.

Does all this sound too far out for you to swallow?

Try a little experiment. Build a fire on a pile of rocks, making sure the rocks have thoroughly dried in the sun so that not a trace of water can be detected on or near them. As the fire gets hotter, you will see the rocks begin to steam. If you listen closely, you can even hear them "cooking." The water was literally in dry storage within the chemical structure of the rocks, prepackaged by God Himself in His provision for a drink of pure water whenever we needed it.

Still not convinced? Look for a minute at some of the many references to "dry water" in the *Manufacturer's Handbook:*

The Lord answered Moses .... "Strike the rock, and water will come out of it for the people to drink."

Exodus 17:5, 6 NIV

The Lord said to Moses.... "Speak to that rock before their eyes and it will pour out its water. You will bring water out of the rock for the community so they and their livestock can drink.

Numbers 20:7, 8 NIV

On that second occasion, Moses goofed, hitting the rock instead of only speaking to it as God had instructed him to do. But God delivered it anyhow, even though Moses missed heaven's best by getting himself into the act. And the water didn't barely trickle out, it gushed. Just look:

Then Moses raised his arm and struck the rock twice with his staff. Water gushed out, and the community and their livestock drank.

Numbers 20:11 NIV

Have you heard scoffers try to discount all that by reasoning that probably the rocks were porous, spongy formations, completely waterlogged? The next time anyone tries that excuse on you, hit him with Deuteronomy 8:15 that tells what kind of rock it was—flint.

Have you ever heard of any spongy flint? Me neither.

Let's look at a few more verses about this amazing phenomenon:

He [God] split the rocks in the desert
    and gave them water as abundant as the seas;
he brought streams out of a rocky crag
    and made water flow down like rivers. . . .

When he struck the rock, water gushed out,
and streams flowed abundantly. . . .

Psalms 78:15, 16, 20 NIV

He opened the rock, and water gushed out;
like a river it flowed in the desert.

Psalms 105:41 NIV

Tremble, O earth, at the presence of the Lord,
at the presence of the God of Jacob,
who turned the rock into a pool,
the hard rock into springs of water.

Psalms 114:7, 8 NIV

. . . he [the Lord] made water flow for them from the rock;
he split the rock and water gushed out.

Isaiah 48:21 NIV

Do you get the picture? Just think how far into the needs of His people God was planning when He stored up unlimited water supplies inside the chemical structure of the geological formations of planet earth. Do you suppose the non-god of evolution could have done all that careful planning? Hardly. It would take a loving Creator God to figure all that out.

And water's not the only thing God stored away to provide essentials for our earth trip. In Deuteronomy 32:13 God says that He made "oil out of the flinty rock." There is an untold abundance of oil contained in shale rock, in a nonliquid state, oil which can be made available through the proper application of heat, though the present state of our technology makes it too costly to produce. But it's there, and by the time we need it, God will have given someone the wisdom to know how to extract it in some way that we can afford.

So much for the creation of the earth and some of the wonders of His provision for oil and water. What about the plants and animals? Let's take a careful look at the Creator's account of how they got here.

5

Presenting the Plant and Animal Kingdoms— Including You

In the beginning, in Genesis 1, the first chapter of the *Manufacturer's Handbook,* we have seen God create light and water and separate the waters above the sky from the waters below the sky. What next? He commanded the waters under the sky to gather into one place so the dry land could show up (Genesis 1:9). He had plans for it!

On the third day of creation, the Creator commanded the dry land to produce vegetation, " '. . . seed-bearing plants and trees on the land that bear fruit with seed in it, according to their various kinds.' And it was so" (Genesis 1:11 NIV).

Everything God commanded in those days was accomplished at once, and God always saw "that it was good." What next? The thing most needful, of course. If all those green plants were to live and not die, they would need sunshine to interact with their chlorophyll to produce food, right? And so the sun and moon were the first order of business on the fourth day.

> And God said, "Let there be lights in the expanse of the sky to separate the day from the night, and let them serve as signs to mark seasons and days and years, and let them . . . give light on the earth." And it was so.
>
> Genesis 1:14, 15 NIV

Fish and birds were next in line. In creating them on the fifth day, God followed the same procedure He had followed with the sun and moon and stars: first He said it, next He did it, and then He saw that it was good:

> And God said, "Let the water teem with living creatures, and let birds fly above the earth across the expanse of the sky." So God created the great creatures of the sea and every living and moving thing with which the water teems, according to their kinds, and every winged bird according to its kind. And God saw that it was good.
>
> Genesis 1:20, 21 NIV

On the same day that He made them, God instructed the creatures in the sea and the winged creatures above the earth to multiply (Genesis 1:22). Where a few days earlier there had been nothing but darkness that was without form and void, business was certainly picking up.

On the sixth day of the beginning of time, again God said it, again God did it, and again God saw that it was good. The first event this time was the creation of living creatures that move along the ground:

"Let the land produce living creatures according to their kinds: livestock, creatures that move along the ground, and wild animals, each according to its kind." And it was so. God made the wild animals according to their kinds, the livestock according to their kinds, and all the creatures that move along the ground according to their kinds. And God saw that it was good.

Genesis 1:24, 25 NIV

Then came the grand finale, the creation of man to run the show. Man didn't show up accidentally, a freak mutant from a hairless ape who also got here by accident, as the evolutionists would have you believe. Man was tailor-made, in the image and likeness of God, to rule over the fish of the sea, the birds of the air, the livestock, and all the creatures that move along the ground—in other words, he was created to rule over all the earth (Genesis 1:26, 27).

Pretty big assignment for a young man just starting out, don't you think? Especially one who was formed from the dust of the ground (Genesis 2:7).

Did I hear a snort of indignation out there somewhere? Look, you skeptics. If *scientists* can turn shoe leather into gold, it's only reasonable to believe that *God* could turn the dust of the ground into Adam. And He didn't have to go through a long evolutionary process, working crossword puzzles while He waited for protozoans to turn into tadpoles, to turn into fish, to turn into lizards, to turn into birds, to turn into monkeys, to turn into people. He could just say it and do it and breathe into His man the breath of life and see that it was good. When He saw something that wasn't good, He fixed it. For instance, when He saw that man had no suitable helper and that it was not good for man to be alone, He made a helper for him out of one of Adam's ribs (Genesis 2:18, 20–22).

I can imagine that by the time the sixth day was ending, God might have surveyed the vast array of things He had made, heaved a great sigh of relief, and said, "Whew! I'm glad that's over!" Quite a feat for six days, inventing the whole creation. So what did Creator God do on the seventh day? He rested, that's what. I don't blame Him, do you?

Before we leave this subject of how God made everything there is, it might be well to tell you, in case you don't know it already, that the first two chapters of the *Manufacturer's Handbook* aren't the only place where the Manufacturer, God, says that He made everything there is. Both the Old Testament and the New have dozens of other Scriptures announcing that God made it all. And there's plenty more where they came from.

... "O Lord, God of Israel. . . . You have made heaven and earth."

2 Kings 19:15 NIV

"Your hands shaped me and made me. . . .
Remember that you molded me like clay. . . ."

Job 10:8, 9 NIV

"When he [God] established the force of the wind
    and measured out the waters,
when he made a decree for the rain
    and a path for the thunderstorm."

Job 28:25, 26 NIV

"The Spirit of God has made me;
    the breath of the Almighty gives me life."

Job 33:4 NIV

When I consider your heavens,
    the work of your fingers,
the moon and the stars,
    which you have set in place,
what is man that you are mindful of him ...?
You made him ruler over the works of your hands ...
all flocks and herds,
    and the beasts of the field,
the birds of the air,
    and the fish of the sea. ...
O Lord, our Lord,
    how majestic is your name in all the earth!

Psalms 8:3, 4, 6–9 NIV

The heavens declare the glory of God;
    the skies proclaim the work of his hands.

Psalms 19:1 NIV

By the word of the Lord were the heavens made,
    their starry host by the breath of his mouth.

Psalms 33:6 NIV

"In the beginning you [God] laid the foundations of the
earth,
and the heavens are the work of your hands."

Psalms 102:25 NIV

How many are your works, O Lord!
    In wisdom you made them all;
    the earth is full of your creatures.

                                        Psalms 104:24 NIV

My help comes from the Lord,
    the Maker of heaven and earth.

                                        Psalms 121:2 NIV

Give thanks to the Lord of lords. . .
    to him who alone does great wonders. . .
    who by his understanding made the heavens. . .
    who spread out the earth upon the waters. . .
    who made the great lights. . .
    the sun to govern the day. . .
    the moon and stars to govern the night. . . .

                                        Psalms 136:3–9 NIV

Blessed is he whose help is the God of Jacob,
    whose hope is in the Lord his God,
the Maker of heaven and earth,
    the sea, and everything in them. . . .

                                        Psalms 146:5, 6 NIV

By wisdom the Lord laid the earth's foundations,
    by understanding he set the heavens in place;
by his knowledge the deeps were divided,
    and the clouds let drop the dew.

                                        Proverbs 3:19, 20 NIV

I [wisdom] was there when he [the Lord] set the heavens in
   place,
      when he marked out the horizon on the face of the
         deep,
   when he established the clouds above
      and fixed securely the fountains of the deep,
   when he gave the sea its boundary
      so the waters would not overstep his command,
   and when he marked out the foundations of the earth.

                                        Proverbs 8:27–29 NIV

Ears that hear and eyes that see—
   the Lord has made them both.

                                        Proverbs 20:12 NIV

Who has measured the waters in the hollow of his hand,
   or with the breadth of his hand marked off the heavens?
Who has held the dust of the earth in a basket,
   or weighed the mountains on the scales
   and the hills in a balance?

                                        Isaiah 40:12 NIV

Lift your eyes and look to the heavens:
   Who created all these?
He who brings out the starry host one by one,
   and calls them each by name. . . .
Do you not know?
   Have you not heard?

The Lord is the everlasting God,
   the Creator of the ends of the earth.

                              Isaiah 40:26, 28 NIV

"This is what the Lord says . . .
I am the Lord,
who has made all things,
who alone stretched out the heavens,
who spread out the earth by myself.

                              Isaiah 44:24 NIV

"It is I [the Lord] who made the earth
   and created mankind upon it. . . ."

                              Isaiah 45:12 NIV

For this is what the Lord says—
he who created the heavens,
   he is God;
he who fashioned and made the earth,
   he founded it;
he did not create it to be empty,
   but formed it to be inhabited. . . .

                              Isaiah 45:18 NIV

"Listen to me, O Jacob . . .
I am he;
   I am the first and I am the last.
My own hand laid the foundations of the earth,
   and my right hand spread out the heavens. . . .

                              Isaiah 48:12, 13 NIV

". . . Who are you . . .
that you forget the Lord your Maker,
who stretched out the heavens
and laid the foundations of the earth. . . ."

Isaiah 51:12, 13 NIV

Yet, O Lord, you are our Father.
We are the clay, you are the potter;
we are all the work of your hand.

Isaiah 64:8 NIV

But God made the earth by his power;
he founded the world by his wisdom
and stretched out the heavens by his understanding.

Jeremiah 10:12 NIV

With my great power and outstretched arm I made the
earth and its people and the animals that are on it. . . .

Jeremiah 27:5 NIV

"He made the earth by his power;
he founded the world by his wisdom
and stretched out the heavens by his understanding."

Jeremiah 51:15 NIV

(He who made the Pleiades and Orion,
who turns blackness into dawn
and darkens day into night,

who calls for the waters of the sea
    and pours them out over the face of the land—
    the Lord is his name—

                       Amos 5:8 NIV

He who builds his lofty palace in the heavens
    and sets its foundation on the earth . . .
    the Lord is his name.

                       Amos 9:6 NIV

This is the word of the Lord. . . . who stretches out the heavens, who lays the foundation of the earth, and who forms the spirit of man within him. . . .

                       Zechariah 12:1 NIV

In the beginning was the Word, and the Word was with God, and the Word was God. He was with God in the beginning.
    Through him all things were made; without him nothing was made that has been made. . . . He was in the world, and though the world was made through him, the world did not recognize him.

                       John 1:1–3, 10 NIV

When they heard this, they raised their voices together in prayer to God. "Sovereign Lord," they said, "you made the heaven and the earth and the sea, and everything in them."

                       Acts 4:24 NIV

" 'Heaven is my throne,
       and the earth is my footstool. . .
       says the Lord. . . .
Has not my hand made all these things?' "

                                        Acts 7:49, 50 NIV

"The God who made the world and everything in it is the
Lord of heaven and earth and does not live in temples
built by hands."

                                            Acts 17:24 NIV

For since the creation of the world God's invisible quali-
ties—his eternal power and divine nature—have been
clearly seen, being understood from what has been made,
so that men are without excuse.

                                          Romans 1:20 NIV

. . . God, who created all things.

                                        Ephesians 3:9 NIV

He is the image of the invisible God, the firstborn over all
creation. For by him all things were created: things in
heaven and on earth, visible and invisible, whether
thrones or powers or rulers or authorities; all things were
created by him and for him.

                                     Colossians 1:15, 16 NIV

For every house is built by someone, but God is the builder of everything.

Hebrews 3:4 NIV

By faith we understand that the universe was formed at God's command, so that what is seen was not made out of what was visible.

Hebrews 11:3 NIV

But they deliberately forget that long ago by God's word the heavens existed and the earth was formed out of water and with water.

2 Peter 3:5 NIV

"You are worthy, our Lord and God,
    to receive glory and honor and power,
for you created all things,
    and by your will they were created
    and have their being."

Revelation 4:11 NIV

"Fear God and give him glory. . . . Worship him who made the heavens, the earth, the sea and the springs of water."

Revelation 14:7 NIV

Looks to me as if a man would be a fool not to believe God knows what He's talking about.

Can *you* believe in evolution? Only if you can call God a liar.

Furthermore, the Scriptures aren't the only place where God says that the the whole creation is His invention. The whole creation says it too. Believe it or not, He has actually "autographed" or "branded" every single plant and animal with something so unique and complex that there is no way it would ever have happened by the accidents of evolution.

"Now, wait just a minute, Hill. That sounds far out to me." My kibitzer is at it again. But this time he's right for a change. It is far out in one sense of the word, I mean it's so fantastic it would take Almighty God to think up a signature so special, so uncounterfeitable by any random chance happenings.

The mark of God's craftsmanship isn't like the scribble stuck in the lower left corner of an ordinary artist's masterpiece. It isn't like the scarred branding-iron label on the walking T-bone chewing grass out in the back pasture. God's DNA "signature" is built into the heart of every single cell of everything alive. Now, since one human body alone is composed of billions of cells, that would be a lot of autographing, wouldn't it? Just thinking about it gives me the worst case of writer's cramp you ever heard of.

Since the Creator's signature is in the heart of every cell, there's no way anyone in his right mind can come along, scribble a scrawl at the base of a giant redwood or pin a label on the monkey cage at the zoo that says, "Made by Evolution."

"But how do you know that God's signature is on every cell?" someone wants to know. I'm glad you asked the question, because the long-ago Psalmist has the answer all lined up for you. Maybe it's a familiar Scripture that you just hadn't thought of literally before. If so, think of it literally now: "O Lord our Lord, how excellent is thy name in all the earth! . . ." (Psalms 8:1). Don't you think that could mean that God has written His excellent name in every crumb of creation, every snowflake even being an original? It's worth thinking about.

Meanwhile, hold on while we take a look through the electron microscope at the amazing ability of the DNA in your cells to keep you going during your life on planet earth.

Every single one of your billions of cells contains a complete manufacturing plant capable of repairing or replacing worn out, destroyed, or damaged parts.[1] Each of these cell factories is controlled by a fantastic computer that science has labeled the DNA molecule.

"DNA? What's that?"

I was just about to tell you. In the first place, DNA is just a nickname—for deoxyribonucleic acid. I don't blame it for going by its nickname, do you? And I think it's significant that DNA spelled backward is AND, because the very specific, exacting instructions contained in the DNA of a single cell would fill one thousand encyclopedia volumes. And every word in them would be spelled with some combination of only four letters (more about that in a minute). Meanwhile, I'll let you figure out for yourself the zillions of zeros in the odds against anything like DNA being invented by accident.

As for what DNA is and what it does, here's an extremely simplified view: DNA is a remarkable God-designed substance which, in combination with protein, makes up the genes on the threadlike chromosomes in the nuclei of almost all cells. DNA is composed of coiled chains of smaller molecules called nucleotides, which are made up of a sugar, a phosphate, and one of four nitrogen-containing bases. The bases are adenine, thymine, guanine, and cytosine—A, T, G, and C, for short—which can be considered the letters of the alphabet for the language of heredity.

These DNA packages, making up your genes, determine everything about your inheritance—your sex, color of skin, eyes, and hair, height, shape, species, and many other inherited characteristics. (More about genes in chapter 8.)

How does DNA work? Let's try a simplified explanation: To begin with, to use modern teenage terminology, A, T, G, and C "go steady." They are never alone, but are always found in A-T or G-C pairs. The pairs can be found in a virtually unlimited variety of orders or arrangements, depending on the job to be done.

For instance, let's suppose you bang your nose against someone's fist. A whole series of new parts are needed for a neat good-as-new repair job—skin cells, blood vessels, flesh, cartilage, sweat glands, and all the rest.

First, Chief DNA would have to call for a whole set of new outer skin. He might do it by giving the following computer command for epidermis to the cell factory: G-C, G-C, A-T, A-T, A-T, G-C, A-T, A-T, A-T, A-T, G-C, G-C, A-T, G-C.

Then Chief DNA might give the computer command for ordering up blood vessels: A-T, A-T, A-T, G-C, G-C, A-T, G-C.

After the Chief had ordered all the necessary supplies, in order to do your nose any good, someone would have to carry out the coded instructions. That's the function of the two RNA boys (ribonucleic acid), who are something like DNA except that they are smaller, have a different kind of sugar, and one base that is different from DNA.

One RNA cell worker is a messenger who travels from the cell's nucleus into the "parts department" containing bins of amino acids; the other RNA cell worker is the technician who supervises assembly of the new material to fix your clobbered proboscis.

The tiniest of errors could turn your face into a disaster area. Suppose the signals from the DNA Chief to the RNA boys got scrambled in the transmission and you wound up with a fingernail growing on the end of your nose instead of a new patch of schnozzle skin. Revolting—and impossible with God's perfect system of programming.

Can man-made computers duplicate this guaranteed perfection? Ask anyone knowledgeable about the subject, and he will say, "Absolutely not." But God never goofs, and when He created every species, He hand-designed their systems for the perpetuation of their own kind. Monkey parts never show up on humans, and fish parts are never seen on birds.

How many billions of years would it take to evolve such a system? Evolution simply answers, "Given enough time, anything can happen and probably will." Proof? They haven't a shred. The next time you have a banged-up nose or a dog-bitten tendon, try to imagine what it would be like if you had to depend on some uncaring universal cosmic force to fix you up. Grim, isn't it? Makes you glad for cells personally autographed with DNA to meet your every need. You might even think of the DNA in your cells as standing for Divine Nature Autographed.

God's perfect system is absolutely goof proof unless tampered with by accident, disease, or human abuse in the form of drugs, chemicals, nuclear radiation, and the like. Only then does it ever grow bad parts from good materials.

"Even a single aspirin tablet, one cigarette, or an ounce of alcohol can injure the unborn child," I read in an article claiming that most birth defects can be traced back to prenatal damage through one of these known causes. The next time you see a deformed child, don't blame the Creator, blame the pushers of such once-perfectly-legal-but-still-lethal wonder drugs as thalidomide.

"But what about cancer?"

Cancer is another type of bad-guy cell not part of God's original good design but one that came about through the "self-will run riot" syndrome, which entered into human nature through the rebellion of its original human daddy. A cancer cell is a physical readout of "I'll do my own thing my own way in my own time if it kills me." It generally does, because by simply descending from Adam, we inherited the obsession to do our own thing instead of following God's instructions. When that attitude shows up in the form of cancer cells, they act to destroy the very body that feeds them.

Doesn't that sound like the philosophy of the world, rebelling against the most high God who created it all and in whose hands is our very life?

In spite of all the evidence pointing to a Creator God in charge of the whole area of genetic engineering, evolution's hold on the human mind is so strong that one writer said:

> Since organisms as different as bacteria, plants, and human beings have the same building blocks for constructing protein, it's possible to combine the genes of . . . an orange with those of an elephant, human genes with those of a grasshopper. This shows that all life forms have been *created* from the same basic genetic material—a fact strongly supporting the theory of *evolution*.[2]

Sounds like double-talk, doesn't it? But that's what you have to expect from folks deceived by an evolutionary frame of mind.

We can't close this chapter without a brief look at the much-discussed, fastest-growing area of scientific research called genetic engineering. GE is based on the theory that all living cells have characteristics enabling them to be joined together to form new types of living organisms. By transferring genes from one DNA to another, combined characteristics show up in ways still unpredictable but which may well eventually change our life on planet earth, for good or ill.

Suppose that an elephant and an orange were to swap some genes, as the article suggested. What would the result be? A pile of oranges at the zoo where you expected to feed Big Jumbo some peanuts? Florida orange groves teeming with elephants on a rampage?

And if humans and grasshoppers suddenly combined forces, imagine the havoc when our genetic code suddenly shouted into our involuntary instinctive motor-control reflex system, "Hey, Hill! There's a bumper crop of wheat out there on the Western prairies! What do you say we get the boys together and go out and destroy it just for kicks?"

Well, the genetic engineering eggheads haven't gone quite that far yet with their "recombinant DNA," as it's called. But they have gone far enough to know that they're playing with fire. Gene swapping just *could* accidentally come up with an uncontrollable strain of bacteria that could wipe us all out. Already there are some laws on the books to establish procedural safeguards in genetic engineering before it's too late.

The whole scene kind of makes you know that future shock is already here, doesn't it? And it puts you on notice that man created in the image of God had better look at what God has done and be careful how he monkeys around with it.

6

But What About Fossils?

"Hey, wait a minute!" I can hear some of you yelling. "But what about all the *proofs* of evolution—the fossils, carbon dating, geology, 'good' mutants, 'gill slits' in human embryos, and all that? And isn't there reliable proof that the earth is actually billions of years old instead of a few thousand years old as the Bible account would have us believe?"

Good questions, worthy of scientific answers.

First, let's look at what the evolutionists themselves have to say about the proofs of their evolutionary theories.[1]

Our first witness is Charles Darwin himself, who says, in his *Origin of the Species:*

As by this theory, innumerable transitional forms must have existed. Why do we not find them imbedded in the crust of the earth? Why is all nature not in confusion instead of being as we see them, well-defined species? Geological research does not yield the infinitely many fine gradations between past and present species required by the theory; and this is the most obvious of the many objections which may be argued against it.

Chalk one up for honesty! Darwin admitted there was no evidence that his theory was correct. Geology was against him. Furthermore, one day he wrote:

> The horrid doubt always arises whether the convictions of man's mind, which has been developed from the mind of the lower animals, are of any value or at all trustworthy. Would anyone trust the convictions of a monkey's mind, if there are any convictions in such a mind? (*Life and Letters,* p. 285).

Darwin wasn't the only one who knew there was no evidence to support the theory of evolution but who believed in it anyway. Listen to some others.

D'Arcy Thompson, biologist, said:

> Eighty years' study of Darwinian evolution has not taught us how birds descend from reptiles, mammals from earlier quadrupeds, quadrupeds from fishes, nor vertebrates from invertebrate stock. We used to be told, and were content to believe, that the old record was of necessity imperfect.... But there is a deeper reason.... A "principle of discontinuity" is inherent in all classifications ... and to seek for stepping stones across the gaps between is to seek in vain, for ever (*On Growth and Form,* p. 1093).

How about that one? Thompson acknowledges that we have *no proof*—and that we never will, even if we look forever.

Le Comte du Nouy, anthropologist, wrote:

> All types of reptiles appear "suddenly" and it is impossible to link them to any terrestrial ancestors. The same is

true of the tortoises. . . . We have no precise facts to go on, and no trace of intermediaries (*Human Destiny,* p. 75).

When *you* have no facts to go on, are you willing to go on without the facts? Might work for some things, but for science?

R.B. Goldschmidt, a geneticist, presents some incontrovertible facts:

Nowhere have the limits of the species been transgressed (*The Material Basis of Evolution,* p. 165, 168). Practically all orders or families known appear suddenly and without any apparent transitions ("Evolution as Viewed by One Geneticist," in the *American Scientist,* Jan. 1952, p. 97). Nobody has ever succeeded in producing a new species, not to mention the higher categories, by selection of micromutations (*Theoretical Genetics,* p. 488).

What did Goldschmidt do with the facts he found? Since they didn't uphold the theory of evolution in which he chose to believe, he bypassed the facts and said that one day a dinosaur egg must have hatched a bird.[2] This is called "the hopeful monster theory," but such reasoning sounds like a hope*less monstrosity* to me.

George Gaylord Simpson, paleontologist, is another who failed to find the proof of evolution in nature. He admitted a deep concern over the absence of certain fossils that ought to have been found if evolution is true. But instead of rejecting evolution, he just called the missing fossils, "The major mystery of life" (*The Meaning of Evolution*). In his *The Principal Factors of Evolution,* Simpson wrote, "We do not find any continuous and progressive succession of traditional forms," and in *Science* for April 22, 1966, he said:

Language is also the most diagnostic single trait of man; all normal men have language; no other now-living organisms do.... Many ... attempts have been made to determine the evolutionary origin of language, but all have failed.

Faced with the facts against evolution, Simpson must have been embarrassed. I would have been. Loren Eiseley, anthropologist, admitted the embarrassment:

With the failure of these many efforts [to create life] science was left in the embarrassing position of having to postulate theories of living origins which it could not demonstrate ... of having to create a mythology of its own: namely, the assumption that what could not be proved to take place today, had, in truth, taken place in the primeval past (*Immense Journey,* p. 199).

His face still red, Eiseley, in *Scientific American* for June, 1956, stated:

For the whole Tertiary Period ... we have to read the story of primate evolution from a few handfuls of broken bones and teeth. These fossils, moreover, are taken from places thousands of miles apart on the Old World land mass.... In the end, we may shake our heads.

Edsel Murphy's Analogs
for Egghead Experimenters:

1. **Nothing ever works as planned. You can depend on it.**

2. You never have the right amount of anything. Too little and too late, or too much and too soon. Or neither.
3. The experiment is always harder than it looks. Thank goodness. If it wasn't, you'd be without excuse for your miserable grade.
4. Never begin an experiment until after you have made up your mind how you want it to turn out.
5. If the experiment works without a hitch, you've used the wrong formula.
6. The stages of an experiment expand to exceed the time allowed. And you're supposed to clean up afterwards.
7. A laboratory collaborator is advisable. You can blame all the explosions on him.
8. Selective gravitation guarantees that toast falls buttered side down on shag rugs, jelly side up on linoleum. But what were you doing eating in the lab?
9. Every experiment is repeatable. It should fail the same way every time. That's the exception that proves the rule.
10. Keep a careful log of results. It will prove you showed up.
11. Never talk about miracles—just depend on them.
12. Your curves will be more uniform if you draw them before your data calculation.
13. When all else fails, consult the directions. Then decide why you know an easier way.

> **14. The amount of equipment absolutely ruined is a fair gauge of the experience gained.**
> **15. If a chemical reaction is slow, turn up the burner and run for your life.**

Well, blushing and headshaking may be good for some-thing, but they don't turn up the proofs needed for evolution to be true. When Eiseley reviewed Jean Rostand's *The Orion Book of Evolution* (1961) in the *New York Times,* he must have shaken his head some more:

> The mutations which we know and which are considered responsible for the creation of the living world, are in gen-eral either organic deprivations, deficiencies, or the dou-bling of pre-existing organs. In any case, they never produce anything really new or original in the organic scheme, nothing which one might consider the basis for a new organ or the priming of a new function. . . .
> No, decidedly, I cannot make myself think that these "slips" of heredity have been able, even with the co-opera-tion of natural selection (and) . . . immense periods of time . . . to build the entire world.

See? Evolutionists themselves admit there is plenty of evi-dence that mutations *can't* do what the evolutionists say they *have* to do for their own theories to be correct. James F. Crow reported, in the *Bulletin of the Atomic Scientists* for January, 1958:

> Mutations and mutation rates have been studied in a wide variety of experimental plants and animals, and in man.

There is one general result that clearly emerges: almost all mutations are harmful (p. 19).

For evolution to work, there must have been many marvelously good mutations, but where are they? The evolutionists can't find them. Have you seen any good mutants walking around lately?

Reviewing biochemistry professor G. A. Kerkut's book, *Implications of Evolution*, James T. Bonner wrote:

This is a book with a disturbing message; it points to some unseemly cracks in the foundations. . . . What is said gives us an uneasy feeling that we knew it for a long time but were never willing to admit this. . . . We have all been telling our students for years not to accept any statement on its face value but to examine the evidence. . . . We have failed to follow our own sound advice. (*American Scientist,* June, 1961, p. 240).

When Saint Paul wrote to the church in Rome, he said, "You teach others—why don't you teach yourself?" (*see* Romans 2:21). That might be a good question for evolutionist professors to ask themselves.

A botanist, R. Good, was getting at honesty when he acknowledged:

There is a steadily growing realization that natural selection is not, and can never have been, the principal cause of evolution it is claimed to be. . . . It depends too much on false parallels and weakly supported assumptions (*The Listener,* May 7, 1959, p. 797).

And Alfred S. Romer, Harvard zoologist, went so far as to say:

Below this (Cambrian strata) are vast thicknesses of sediments in which the progenitors . . . would be expected. But we do not find them; these older beds are almost barren of life, and the general picture *could reasonably be consistent with the idea of special creation*. . . . (*Natural History,* October, 1959).

I bet Romer almost got excommunicated from the evolutionary fraternity for that one. In another place, he lamented:

Links are missing just where we most fervently desire them, and it is all too probable that many "links" will continue to be missing.

Before you get all dressed up to help Romer celebrate with a gigantic pity party about the missing links, take a gander at what some evolutionists did about that situation. Not satisfied with missing links, they chose to *supply* them, in some of the greatest hoaxes ever perpetrated on the "scientific" world.

I quote from Ray Smith's "The Folly of Evolution" in the August–September, 1974, issue of the *Bible-Science Newsletter* again:

**Edsel Murphy Egghead Analog:
Uncertainty—Rooting through the wreckage in
search of a reasonable alibi.**

Looking at exhibits in museums and at pictures in school textbooks, one would think that evolutionists had found complete skulls and skeletons of ape-men and that it is a proven fact that man ascended from the apes. Truthfully, no complete skulls or skeletons of what may honestly be called ape-men have been found. With a piece of skull, a jawbone and a few fragments, the evolutionist can produce an ape-man with all details. This is hardly honest procedure. Some of these specimens have been found to be frauds.

In 1912 near Piltdown, England, Charles Dawson and Arthur Keith discovered what they claimed was an ape-man. Sir Arthur Woodward and Teilhard de Chardin came to assist in the work. From a skull, a jawbone having teeth, and a few fragments they constructed Piltdown man which was exhibited for 41 years in the British Museum as an authentic ape-man. In 1953 John Winer and Samuel Oakley, after a long and close examination, found that the skull was of modern man, that the jawbone was that of an ape, that the teeth had been filed to look ape-like, and that the jawbone had been treated with bichromate of potassium and "salt of iron" to give it the appearance of being fossilized. . . .

E. Dubois, a Dutch surgeon, created a sensation when he announced that he had found Java man at Sumatra in Indonesia. He named it Pithecanthropus, which means ape-man. . . . After a thorough investigation, a group of German paleontologists pronounced Pithecanthropus a man, not an ape-man. Dubois admitted the remains were not those of an ape-man and that he had found remains of modern man in the same place.

In 1959 Dr. Louis B. Leakey announced that he had found the remains of a primitive man in Africa, and he named him Zinjanthropus. He first dated him at 600,000 years, but later (by using the Potassium/Argon method) gave him an age of more than one million years. Before his death in 1972, Dr. Leakey admitted that the skull was that of an ape. In spite of these frauds, we are asked to have implicit faith in the evolutionist who is often more a philosopher than a scientist, who is sometimes in error, and sometimes is even dishonest.

According to an article in *Discover* magazine, Leakey's son is carrying on in the family tradition. Hear this from a review of his *The Making of Mankind* on page 84 of the August, 1981, issue of *Discover:*

> But good genes and vast experience contribute less toward making Richard Leakey an effective popularizer of paleoanthropology than does his fearless ability to draw sweeping conclusions about early man based on little hard evidence—a sprinkling of telltale hominid fossils and not many more artifacts. As Leakey admits, "Facts have often been in short supply in the study of human prehistory."

Can you imagine "scientists" faking the evidence to support their shaky theories? Or admitting that their theories are based on "facts" more notable for their absence than their presence? Science is supposed to stand on fact, not on crutches of make-believe and "Let's pretend."

Hand in hand with the deceptions of the fabricators of "missing links" goes one of the weirdest science-fiction type theories still being pushed on an uninformed public. Called the "recapitulation theory," it goes something like this: "Every human child born into this world starts out in a single-cell embryonic state, and then, through a series of changes, becomes an infant."

All okay so far. No argument. But get a load of this further rundown: "The changes in the development of the embryo exactly duplicate all the stages represented by the Darwinian concept of protozoan-to-people, and each stage is clearly discernible in the developing embryo. The single cell changes into a fish, complete with gill slits, the fish becomes a lizard, the lizard changes into a bird, the bird into an ape, and thus into a people."

Have you swallowed all that? And doesn't it make you glad that you weren't born three months ahead of schedule? You might have wound up in the zoo with the other simians instead of in a cradle at your parents' house.

This theory, sometimes called the "biogenetic law," was dreamed up by a zoologist named Haeckel. It is still taught in many institutions of so-called higher learning. "Ontogeny (the development of an organism) recapitulates phylogeny (the evolution of a group of organisms)," Haeckel said.

Using untruth as a foundation for his theories, Haeckel became famous for what the *Encyclopaedia Britannica* calls his "confident construction of genealogical trees of living organisms." He wrote books, delivered learned addresses at important scientific meetings, and denied God. According to the *Britannica,* "Darwin believed that Haeckel's enthusiastic propagation of the doctrine of organic evolution was the chief factor in the success of the doctrine in Germany." In his day, he was widely read and loudly acclaimed. But when the truth came out, and it was proven that he had falsified some of the evidence on which he hung his theory, he went down in history, way down. How would you like to be written up in the *EB* this way:

Haeckel occupies no serious position in the history of philosophy, and it can be held that in the formulation of his ideas he was somewhat unscrupulous in his treatment of scientific facts.... Haeckel was an excellent artist but tended to be led by his imagination.

Translated into plain English, someone who is "somewhat unscrupulous in his treatment of scientific facts" is a liar, and a scientist whose substantiating drawings are things he made up in his own head—well, I'll let you name him. But if such a man told me it was raining, I'd be a fool to open my umbrella without first checking it out for myself. When the truth is on your side, you don't have to fake anything.

Let's look at what one scientist says about Haeckel's "evidence."

Probably one of the most widespread of the recapitulation fallacies concerns the fact that at a particular stage of development, the human embryo possesses (as do the embryos of many mammals) structures which superficially resemble the gills of fish. These embryonic features, erroneously referred to as "gill pouches" or "gill slits," are then said to "repeat or recapitulate a fish stage in our evolution."

However, this is most certainly not the case. It is true that a series of five alternating ridges and grooves are present in mammalian embryos in approximately the same region as the gill bars of aquatic vertebrates such as fish. In fish these grooves open into the pharynx, forming the true gill slits through which water passes for respiration. In mammals, birds, and reptiles, however, these structures never function in respiration, nor are there ever any openings into the pharynx. Moreover, in mammals these pharyngeal bars (as they are more properly termed) begin immediately to undergo further development. . . . The first arch and its pouch [i.e., groove] . . . form the upper and lower jaws and inner ear of higher vertebrates. The second, third, and fourth arches contribute to the tongue, tonsils, parathyroid gland, and thymus.

None of these structures, it may be noted, are associated with respiration. Thus, the use of the biogenetic "law" to support the fish ancestry of mammals and other non-aquatic vertebrates has no basis in fact ("Perpetuation of the Recapitulation Myth," by Glen W. Wolfrom, *Creation Research Society Quarterly,* March, 1975, p 199).

So-called gill slits proving that people came from fish? Makes about as much sense as saying that candy canes come from zebras. Only suckers would buy reasoning like that.

If the evolutionists themselves express doubts that their case could hold up in court, and even stoop to the deceit of inventing false evidence, what do the *real* scientists say, the men who carefully examine and consider all the true evidence—pro and con—before reaching a conclusion? Just as you would expect, they find the evolutionists guilty of gross stupidity, blindness, and conclusions not supported by any facts, only by figments of their imaginations. Listen fast to a few *real* scientists:

"If the human eye came by chance, then so could a telescope!" (William Paley, famous naturalist, 1743–1805).

"The theories of evolution with which our studious youth have been deceived, constitute a dogma that all the world continues to teach; but each man in his specialty, the zoologist or the botanist, ascertains that none of the explanations furnished is adequate" (Paul Lemoine, in *Encyclopedie Francaise,* V, pp. 82–83, 1937).

"Natural selection, contrary to what Darwin held, has a conserving effect, and *limits* the variability of species" (Emile Guyenot, in *Encyclopedie Francaise,* V, pp. 82–83, 1937).

"It is impossible for scientists any longer to agree with Darwin's theory of the origin of species. After forty years, no evidence has been discovered to verify his genesis of species. . . .

Even time cannot complete that which has not yet begun" (Sir William Bateson, famous geneticist, 1921).

"No matter how far back we go into the fossil record . . . we find no trace of any animal forms intermediate between the major groups or phyla. . . . It is a fair supposition that there never have been any such intergrading types.

"There is not the slightest evidence that any of the major groups of animals arose from each other. Each is a special animal complex . . . appearing, therefore, as a special distinct creation" (Austin H. Clark, U.S. Museum of Natural History, in *The New Evolution: Zoogenesis,* pp. 189–196).

"The most unexpected part of the paleontological evidence remains to be mentioned: the further back we look for early man, the more like ourselves he appears to be" (Dr. Rendle Short, surgeon, in *The Victoria Institute,* p. 10).

"The facts . . . do not support the notion of a beast-like early man" (M.F.A. Montagy, renowned anthropologist, in *Introduction to Physical Anthropology*).

"My attempt to demonstrate evolution by an experiment carried on for more than forty years, has completely failed. . . . It is not even possible to make a caricature of an evolution out of paleo-biological facts. The fossil material is now so complete that . . . the lack of transitional series cannot be explained as due to the scarcity of the material. The deficiencies are real, they will never be filled. The idea of evolution rests on pure belief!" (Heribert Nilsson, Director of Botany Inst., Lund Univ., in *Synthetische Artbildung,* Vol. I & II, 1953 [trans.]).

"Extreme evolutionism in its various forms is an obstacle to scientific progress, because it leads those who hold it to misconceive their problems and misinterpret the data they observe. If biology is to advance, this theory should be abandoned even as a working hypothesis" (G.H. Duggan, philosopher, in *Evolution & Philosophy*).

"As we know, there is a great divergence of opinion among biologists, not only about the causes of evolution but even about the actual process. This divergence exists because the evidence is unsatisfactory and does not permit any certain conclusion. . . . We now know that the variations determined by environmental changes . . . regarded by Darwin as the material on which natural selection acts—are not hereditary. . . . The success of Darwinism was accompanied by a decline in scientific integrity. The modern Darwinian paleontologists are obliged, just like their predecessors and like Darwin, to water down the facts with subsidiary hypotheses which are in the nature of things unverifiable." (W. R. Thompson, director, Commonwealth Inst. of Biological Control, in his introduction to *The Origin of Species,* Everyman's Library Edition, E. P. Dutton & Co., 1956.)

"The probability of life originating from accident is comparable to the probability of the unabridged dictionary resulting from an explosion in a printing shop" (Edwin Conklin, biologist, Princeton Univ., in *Reader's Digest,* January, 1963).

"To the unprejudiced, the fossil record of plants is in favor of special creation" (E. J. H. Corner, botanist, Cambridge Univ., in *Contemporary Botanical Thought*).

"Mutations deal only with changes in existing characters, never with the appearance of a new functioning character. . . . And yet it is the appearance of new characters in organisms which marks the boundaries of the major steps in the evolutionary scale" (H. Graham Cannon in *The Evolution of Living Things*).

"All of our experience shows that contrary to what Darwin believed, the variability potential of each species is definitely limited" (Walter E. Lammerts, director of research, Germain's Horticultural Research Division, in *Discoveries Since 1859 Which Invalidate the Evolution Theory,* Creation Research Society Annual, 1964).

"Scientists who go about teaching that evolution is a fact of life are great con men, and the story they are telling may be the greatest hoax ever. In explaining evolution, we do not have one iota of fact" (T. N. Tahmisian, physiologist, U.S. Atomic Energy Commission).

"Protoplasm evolving a universe is a superstition more pitiable than paganism" (President Leavitt of Lehigh University).

A summary of evidence against evolution is presented by George F. Howe:

"1. Complex forms often appear before simpler ones. 2. 'Advanced' and 'primitive' characters occur in the same plant. 3. Modern forms are often identical to remote fossil specimens. 4. Where phylogenies (family trees) are postulated, significant gaps occur. 5. Characters thought to belong to one group are found distributed in other unrelated groups. 6. Angiosperm [flowering plant] ancestry has remained a complete mystery" (George F. Howe, biologist, in *Paleobotanical Evidences for a Philosophy of Creationism,* Creation Research Society Annual, 1964).

"The various evidences which evolutionists cite to support their religion can be understood equally well, in fact better, in terms of creation. For example, those evidences based on superficial resemblances, such as comparative anatomy, embryo development, blood sera, and the like, give strong testimony not to evolutionary kinships, but rather to their creation by a common Designer who used similar structures and patterns to accomplish similar . . . functions.

"The fossil record of former life on earth has essentially the same great unbridged gaps between the basic kinds of creatures that exist in the modern world. There is thus no genuine evidence of evolution at all!" (Henry M. Morris, hydrologist, in *Evolution, the Established Religion of the State*).

The list of credible quotations could go on and on. There is no proof that evolution is true, plenty of evidence that it can't be. But evolutionists continue to put on their blinders, stop up their blushing ears, and bury their shaking heads in the sand.

Goldschmidt, quoted earlier, tries to get around the lack of evidence by saying, "Evolution of the animal and plant world is considered by *all those entitled to judgment* to be a fact for which no further proof is needed" (*American Scientist,* v. 40, p. 84). Goldschmidt's definition of those entitled to judgment must be confined to those who say, "Please don't confuse me with the facts. My mind is made up."

Julian Huxley, biologist, first director-general of UNESCO, proclaimed, at the Darwin Centennial Celebration, "No serious scientist would deny that evolution has occurred" (*Evolution After Darwin,* vol. 3, p. 41). His definition of a "serious scientist" is the same sinking ship with Goldschmidt's definition of "those entitled to judgment."

Evolutionist George Wald, professor of biology at Harvard University, makes this profound pronouncement:

"The most complex machine man has ever devised—say an electronic brain—is child's play compared with the simplest of living organisms. . . . One has only to contemplate . . . to concede that the spontaneous generation of a living organism is impossible. Yet here we are—as a result, I believe, of spontaneous generation. . . . Time is in fact the hero of the plot. . . . One has only to wait: time itself performs the miracles" (*The Physics and Chemistry of Life,* p. 9–12, Scientific American, Inc.).

Wald says that one has only to think to know it can't be so, and then he says he believes it anyway. Is that the mark of a true scientist?

Over and over again, evolutionists are found saying that "all true scientists," "all reputable biologists," "most enlightened persons" agree with them, when in fact, the exact opposite is true. "It takes one to know one," is an old adage that might explain what has happened here. A phony scientist, one who ignores the facts that disprove his theory, isn't equipped to recognize the genuine article.

In 1 Timothy 6:20, Saint Paul warned us against phony scientists. We should have listened when he said:

O Timothy, keep that which is committed to thy trust, avoiding profane and vain babblings, and oppositions of science falsely so called.[3]

Ray Smith's article, "The Folly of Evolution," already quoted in part, raises other interesting questions about the fixity of species, and cites further proof that evolution can't possibly be the answer to how it all began:

If present living forms evolved from primitive unicellular forms, why are there still millions of unicellular protozoa in that primitive state living today? Why have they not evolved to a higher state? Also, why are there 15,000 kinds of protozoa living today? If they derived from the first protozoan, why have they remained unicellular and primitive?

Evolutionists date the corals at 500 million years. Why does a close examination of corals show little, if any, change? . . .

The Tuatara is the only one of its reptilian order alive today. Its fossils are dated from the Cretaceous era, but there is no evident difference between the fossils and the living Tuatara, supposedly 135 million years later. The coelacanth has protuberances with fins on the end. When evolutionists first found fossils of this fish, they said the protuberances were growing legs and that later the fins disappeared. It was claimed the fish had become extinct 300 million years ago. However, some live coelacanth have been caught, and it is noted that the growing legs have not grown and the fins have not disappeared and are still used for swimming.

The capillary tree known as the Gingko or Gingko biloba is dated from the Jurassic era, but after "150 million years" this tree grows in Japan unchanged throughout all these centuries. . . .

Evolution maintains that less complex beings preceded more complex beings. The virus is far less complex than a living cell, but being a parasite, the virus could not live without a hostess cell, and therefore, could not have preceded it. On the other hand, some viruses reproduce every half-hour, making it possible for scientists to observe 17,500 generations within ten years. In all the years of studying the virus, no major mutations have been observed. . . .

Well, we began this chapter with Darwin, let's close it with him on a very different note from the one on which we began. From somewhere there came into my hands a little tract about Brother Darwin, written by one Oswald J. Smith and published by the Gospel Tract Society of Independence, Missouri. In the tract he quoted a story told by Lady Hope, a Christian from Northfield, England. Fasten your seat belts again while we travel together to some shoutin' ground. I'll give it to you in the lady's own words:

It was one of those glorious autumn afternoons that we sometimes enjoy in England, when I was asked to go in and sit with the well-known professor, Charles Darwin. He was almost bedridden for some time before he died. I used to feel when I saw him that his fine presence would have made a grand picture for our Royal Academy; but never did I think so more strongly than on this one particular occasion.

He was sitting up in bed, wearing a soft embroidered dressing gown of rather a rich purple shade. Propped up by pillows, he was gazing out on a far-stretching scene of woods and cornfields, which glowed in the light of a marvelous sunset. His noble forehead and fine features seemed to be lit with pleasure as I entered the room.

He waved his hand toward the window as he pointed out the scene beyond, while in the other hand he held an open Bible, which he was always studying.

"What are you reading now?" I asked as I was seated by his bedside. "Hebrews!" he answered—"still Hebrews, The Royal Book, I call it." Then placing his finger on certain passages, he commented on them.

I made some allusions to the strong opinion expressed by many persons on this history of the Creation, its grandeur, and then their treatment of the earliest chapters of the Book of Genesis.

He seemed greatly distressed, his fingers twitched nervously, and a look of agony came over his face as he said, "I was a young man with unformed ideas. I threw out queries, suggestions, wondering all the time over everything; and to my astonishment the ideas took like wildfire. People made a religion of them."

Then he paused, and after a few more sentences on "the holiness of God" and "the grandeur of the Book," looking at the Bible, which he was holding tenderly all this time, he suddenly said, "I have a summer house in the garden which holds about thirty people. It is over there," pointing through the open window. "I want you very much to speak there. I know you read the Bible in villages. Tomorrow afternoon I should like the servants on the place, and a few of the neighbors to gather there. Will you speak to them?"

"What shall I speak about?" I asked. "Jesus Christ!" he replied, "and His salvation. Is that not the best theme?"

How about that? Sounds to me as if Darwin repented of his vain philosophy in time to make it to the pearly gates and life forever with His Creator God. It just goes to show that there's hope for us all.

7

And What About Carbon Dating—And All That?

"But what about carbon dating and all that?" someone's hollering. "Don't those things prove that plants and animals have to be a whole lot older than the Bible says they are?"

All right, let's take a look at those things and see what they say and see how they fit in with what science is discovering.

You have no doubt heard lots of conflicting theories about the age of our personal spacecraft called planet earth. Some people claim that its age runs into billions of years. Others, those who believe the Bible account, will tell you the real age of the earth is closer to ten thousand years. Still others have in-between numbers that they believe to be the true answer. All of these folks are sincere in their beliefs, but with such a wide variation in numbers, some of them just have to be sincerely wrong.

Maybe you've been told that the "clock in the rock" dating system, using the half-life principle of radioactive isotopes, such as Carbon-14, tells the whole story. Well it doesn't. But since determining the age of fossil remains of once-living creatures is such an important matter for evolutionists and creationists let's see how Carbon-14 dating works—and how it doesn't work. In the following passage from his "The Folly of Evolution" (*Bible-Science Newsletter,* August–September, 1974), Ray Smith describes and evaluates this method:

> The C-14 method . . . was invented by Dr. Libby (1947) who was given the Nobel Prize. Plants get their carbon from the atmosphere, and animals get their carbon from the plants they eat. Most of the carbon in the atmosphere is C-12 which is stable and keeps its identity. C-14 is an isotope of carbon and is less abundant. An isotope . . . emits rays and is radioactive. This radioactivity changes C-14 into nitrogen. In a period of 5730 years, one-half of a given quantity of C-14 is changed into nitrogen. As a living being takes in no more carbon after his death, scientists believe they can calculate the time of its death with a Geiger counter.
>
> There are some things which make this method questionable. We cannot be sure of the amount of C-14 present at the time of the death. We are not sure that the C-14 in the atmosphere was always stable. C-14 is produced by cosmic rays bombarding nitrogen at high altitudes in the atmosphere. These bombardments may be caused by what are commonly called the "Northern Lights" (Aurora borealis) and by the sunspots which sometimes cover as much as one-sixth of the sun's surface. How does this affect the amount of C-14 in the atmosphere? How much C-14 is lost by filtration? Scientists tell us that the magnetic fields of the poles have changed at some time, and this would also affect the amount of C-14 in the atmosphere.
>
> In Siberia frozen mammoths have been found in the ice

with tropical vegetation, partly digested, in their stomachs. In Alaska there are great quantities of oil and remains of semi-tropical animals, and in western United States dinosaur remains have been found. It is claimed the largest dinosaurs ate as much as 1000 pounds of food per day. All this indicates that at one time the earth had a universal tropical climate and tropical vegetation. How would this affect C-14? . . .

Having established the uncertainty of Carbon-14 dating, Smith goes on to point out other disadvantages of the C-14 method for the evolutionists' theories:

In a giant international enterprise in which over 90 universities and museums collaborated, more than 15,000 remains of what were once living beings were dated by the revised method of C-14. The results were published in the annual magazine *Radiocarbon*. Here are some results: one Neanderthal man 32,000 years and another 40,000 years. Coal formerly dated at 200 to 300 million years dated at 1680 years. Rhodesian man or "Broken Hill" man dated at 9000 years and bones of Thamesville and Catham, Ontario, dated at 8900 years. Mammiferous bones found at the same site where Dr. Leakey found his "hominid skull" which he claimed was at least 600,000 years old, were given an age of 10,000 years. Bones from the Omo Valley of Ethiopia which were said to have been older than those found by Dr. Leakey were given an age of only 15,000 years. Notice nothing is dated at more than 40,000 years.

By evolutionists' standards 40,000 years is but a passing moment in time. We have already seen that, by their own admission, their theory requires an earth that is millions, if not billions, of years old. Certainly the results of Carbon-14 dating do not offer them much support.

Edsel Murphy Egghead Analog:
Circular Reasoning——A device used by evolutionists to impress one another and to mislead everybody else. E.g.,

> Q.: "How old is this fossil?"
> A.: "At least a billion years old."
> Q.: "How do you know?"
> A.: "Because it was found in a strata at least a billion years old."
> Q.: "How do you know the strata is that old?"
> A.: "Because it contained a fossil at least a billion years old."

The Potassium-Argon series is another sophisticated method of dating; it comes up with an earth about 4.5 billion years old.

Just how accurate are these radiometric methods of dating rocks and fossils? Are Carbon-14, the Potassium-Argon series, and related methods reliable in any degree? With so many conflicting stories in circulation, it's no wonder most folks stay confused. Let's check out a few more specific examples of actual results arrived at by proponents of such "exact" measurements.

Writing in *Science,* Keith and Anderson reported that, using the Carbon-14 dating system, a living mollusk was "proven" to be 3,000 years old. Probably came as quite a surprise to the clam—or whatever mollusk it was—to find that he was eligible for the *Guinness Book of World Records* (*Science*, 141:634, 1963).

Lava samples taken from a volcano which erupted in Hawaii in 1801 showed an age of nearly 3 billion years when tested by the Potassium-Argon dating method (*Journal of Geophysical Research*, 73:4601, July, 1968).

According to evolutionists, the dinosaur died out about 70 million years ago, long before man ever came on the scene. A recent discovery has caused much embarrassment: human footprints alongside dinosaur tracks near the Paluxy River in Texas (*see* the report by Kelly Segraves, *The Great Dinosaur Mistake* [San Diego, Calif.: Beta Books], pp. 34–39).

Samples of moon rock, brought back by our astronauts, were evaluated by various radiometric techniques in our best-equipped laboratories, by our most highly skilled technicians. The results? Readings varied all the way from 700 million years to 28 billion years, according to John G. Read in *Scientific Representations* (P.O. Box 2384, Culver City, Calif. 90230). But look with me for a minute at what that would mean.

When NASA began planning for our first moon walk, much concern was expressed over the "fact" that the layer of dust covering the moon might swallow up the first astronaut who landed there. Evolutionists insisted that due to the large volume of dust being dumped on that heavenly body each year, based on the 14,300,000 tons estimated to be falling annually on planet earth (*Scientific American*, February, 1960, p. 132), after 5 billion years (their estimate of the age of the moon), the coating of dust on the moon would be 137 feet deep! (*See* Kofahl & Segraves, *The Creation Explanation* [Wheaton, Ill.: Harold Shaw Publishers] pp. 190, 195.)

Just how deep was the moon dust as reported by Astronaut Neil Armstrong? Just about one-eighth of an inch.

If our own planet were anywhere close to 5 billion years old, wouldn't we be wallowing around in a sea of meteoric dust 137 feet deep? Even the mere 4.5-million-year earth age suggested by the McGraw Hill *Encyclopedia of Science and Technology* (6:151) would mean much discomfort and sneezies as we kicked up all that space dust blanketing our planet.

No matter how you figure, you can't prove that the planet earth is an elderly lady on her last legs. All valid tests indicate than an age in the neighborhood of ten thousand years is a lot closer to the truth.

"Isn't there any reliable measurement available to folks who believe in the Bible account?" someone's asking. I'm glad you asked. God just happened to design into the earth system a method of measurement that coincides with His biblical account of the whole affair. The most reliable, easily observable and completely repeatable system for measuring the age of planet earth is based on magnetism. It is called the earth's magnetic moment, which is simply a way of referring to the strength of the earth's magnet.

Almost everyone knows that the earth has a north pole and a south pole, but not everyone has realized that the word *pole* refers also to the two magnetic poles of the earth. These poles are so strong that no matter where you are, a compass needle will point toward the north pole.

What causes this huge earth magnet to keep on acting like one? Doesn't it require a lot of power to keep it functioning? And how does it work? Yes, it requires a lot of power, and here's how it works.

Down inside the earth is a molten metal core around which a circulating current flows continuously, round and round. When an electical current flows around a metal core, a magnet is the result. Maybe you remember trying this in a high school science class—winding a number of turns of small wire around an iron nail and connecting it to a dry-cell battery. The nail becomes a magnet and stays that way as long as current flows through the wire. Disconnect the wire so that the current stops flowing, and the magnetic force stops happening.

In the case of the earth, the current flows on and on. No one pulls the plug. The resulting magnetism is important for many things, which we won't go into here, other than enabling us to arrive at the age of the earth. How? Hang on and we'll see.

A professor of physics at the University of Texas at El Paso came up with an expanded version of a theory called "Lamb's Theory." He showed that the magnetic moment, or strength of the earth's magnetic system, should decay or diminish in an orderly and uniform "exponential" manner that is fully predictable over any interval of time.

All that means is that every year, the magnetic strength of our planet's system is less than it was the year before, enabling us to calculate the age of this planet by measuring the magnetic force today and comparing it with what was there in the beginning. This is done by "extrapolation," which is an egghead way of saying, "We measure it backward."

Back in 1835, a German physicist named K. F. Gauss measured the earth's magnetic moment, or field strength. Because of his work, the name Gauss has been given to the lines of force in a magnetic system. Since his measurements, others have measured as well, all of them indicating that the magnetism of planet earth is on an orderly downward trend. Data collected indicates the half-life decay rate of earth's magnetic moment at 1,400 years, while the electrical energy required to keep the earth's magnet running is decreasing at a half-life rate of only 700 years.

"What is all this about half-life?" some of you are asking. Here's an explanation so simple that even I can understand it. Let's assume that you have a gallon of magnetism. Never have seen a gallon of magnetism? Neither have I, but a hypothetical gallon will work just as well as a real one for our illustration. According to the half-life principle, the magnetic material will "go away" or decay at a constant rate, which in the case of magnetism is 1,400 years. That means that at the end of every 1,400 years, the magnet will be only half as strong as it was at the beginning of the 1,400-year period. At the end of the second 1,400-year period, half of the remaining half would be gone, and so on, until it was all used up.

If we wrote down as a mathematical formula what would happen in 14,000 years (ten times 1,400), the formula would look like this:

$$1 \times .5 \times .5 \times .5 \times .5 \times .5 \times .5 \times .5 \times .5 \times .5 \times .5 = .0009765 \text{ or } 1/1024$$

The 1 represents the amount we started with, the whole amount of magnetism that was here in the beginning, and the 1/1024 is the amount that would be left after 14,000 years.

"Why, that would be so nearly nothing, you could hardly measure it—our bucket would be empty for all practical purposes," someone says. That's right. And if our earth were billions of years old, as the evolutionists insist, and if the magnetic moment had always followed a decay rate of 1,400 years per half-life, there would be no measurable magnetism left. In fact, even if the earth's age is only 14,000 years, our present magnetic moment would be far weaker than we observe it to be. How do we account for that?

Remember that First Law of Thermodynamics that says energy can neither be created nor destroyed? It's still a factor in the picture. So where did the magnetism go when it was used up under the half-life principle? It shows up in the form of heat. As the earth's magnetism diminishes, the earth heats up, at a measurable rate. Keep that in mind as we do a little further exploration.

The electrical energy system inside the earth that furnishes battery power to run the big magnet is decreasing at a half-life rate of 700 years. If we go back in history just 7,000 years—ten half-lives of the decay rate of its electrical power system, we arrive at a magnetic energy value 1,024 times what we can measure today. If we go back 28,000 years, at the same exponential rate of decay, the formula would call for 40 half-lives of 7,000 years each, amounting to trillions of times the amount of magnetism we can handle? Why? Read on.

Keep in mind that magnetic decay produces heat, and large-number magnetic decay produces great amounts of heat. As this heat shows up in the structure of the earth, it will dissipate harmlessly as infrared energy escaping to outer space. But if the rate of heating exceeds the earth's ability to dissipate it, overheating results, in much the same manner as your car radiator in standstill traffic in the hot sun. Something has to go. Generally, a radiator hose bursts to relieve the steam pressure built up inside the engine.

It works the same way with the earth's cooling system. If too much energy is built up over too long a period of time, something has to give. Let's look at what would happen if the earth were even 30,000 years old. In order to arrive at our present magnetic energy level, based on the 7,000-year half-life principle, the rate of magnetic decay over the intervening years would have been so intense, the entire earth would have melted long ago. We would be dealing with numbers over a trillion times the values arrived at by scientific observation. These are facts and not theories, and are provable by instruments called magnetometers, which oil exploration people use in determining the life of oil wells.

Studies of the whole matter since Gauss began his measurements early in the last century indicate that an earth age anything like the 4.5 billion years suggested by evolutionists would be completely ridiculous. It just couldn't work that way. An earth age of 10,000 years, on the other hand, fits neatly into the numbers arrived at in the real world of working scientists.

"But how do you reconcile those six days of creation with your ten-thousand-year earth-age theory?" someone wants to know. "Isn't it true that those days were actually a thousand years long?"

Not the way I figure it. Genesis 1:12 says that God created the vegetable kingdom—trees, grasses, crops, and greenery—on the third day. There were trees loaded with fruit, all ready to eat, fruit with seeds inside them for further crops for future generations. Any student of freshman biology can tell you that the vegetable kingdom needs to be fed, that plants make their own food through a process known as photosynthesis. When the sunlight strikes green leaves, sugar is manufactured, and the plant grows, the fruit trees prosper, and kids get apples to eat.

What if the vegetable kingdom was created and then had to wait a thousand years for the sunshine with its actinic rays—not found in all kinds of light, but abundant in sunshine—so plants could make their food? What would have happened during that long, dark waiting period? How long do you think a green tree, plant, flower, or bush could live without food? Certainly not a thousand years, right? But that's exactly what those one thousand-years-equal-one-day-in-creation folks are asking us to believe—that those poor plants had to fast for a thousand years before they could get fed and start to grow. What a hunger trip that would have been, waiting a thousand years for Big Mac to open for business.

Can you imagine what would have happened to all those

trees and plants if each day of creation had been only one year long—or even a few months? Total disaster. Every sign of the newly created vegetable kingdom would have vanished before the sun ever came out.

I've found it makes the best kind of sense to take God at His Word and believe that each day in the Genesis account of creation was a literal day, twenty-four hours long. You can turn away from eggheaditis and join me if you choose.

Any way you look at it, all scientific signs are pointing to the fact that planet earth is on its last legs, so to speak, and that "the end of all things is at hand" (1 Peter 4:7), just as God states in His *Manufacturer's Handbook.*

In order to explain away some of the unavoidable conclusions of the "magnetic moment," some evolutionists have come up with a theory that "magnetic reversals" took place many times over the billions of years of earth history. But they have no proof that their theory is correct. A mechanism that causes magnetic rocks to change polarity is apparently totally unrelated to this theory, leaving the evolutionists as out on a limb as they were when the Piltdown man was discovered to be a clever hoax.

There's another egghead concept, the dynamo theory, which says the earth operates like a giant dynamo or electric generator. But the provision eggheads make for all the billions of horsepower needed to turn the theoretical armature within the magnetic field to produce all those billions of amperes circulating inside the core is just as nonexistent as the first little wiggly in the glob of goo with which they propose to start all life on the earth. You can buy their theory if you want to, but it is entirely without support in simple engineering principles. More holey than holy, too.

After considering all the earth-dating options, I've decided that magnetism provides the only valid, observable, repeatable, measurable means of charting the descent of earth's energy system toward that eventual bottom line called "heat death," where all systems stop functioning as total entropy sets in. But nothing is ever bad news for King's kids. Because at that lowest point, Jesus will come back and step in to bring glory ever after. Here's how He puts it in 2 Peter 3:10–14:

> But the day of the Lord will come as a thief in the night; in the which the heavens shall pass away with a great noise, and the elements shall melt with fervent heat, the earth also and the works that are therein shall be burned up. Seeing then that all these things shall be dissolved, what manner of persons ought ye to be in all holy conversation and godliness, Looking for and hasting unto the coming of the day of God, wherein the heavens being on fire shall be dissolved, and the elements shall melt with fervent heat? Nevertheless we, according to his promise, look for new heavens and a new earth, wherein dwelleth righteousness. Wherefore, beloved, seeing that ye look for such things, be diligent that ye may be found of him in peace, without spot, and blameless.

I don't know about you, but if I'm still hanging around earth when that great and glorious day arrives, I want to be ready to go to live with Him in that new heaven.

8

But What About Hybrids?

"But what about hybrids like corn, in which the offspring could be labeled 'improved' over the original parent stock? And what about other kinds of improvements that researchers can plan for and see with their own eyes? Don't they prove that evolution works?"

I'm glad you asked the question. It's another good one that deserves an answer.

Actually, hybrids *disprove* evolution, because the seed of the hybrid does not reproduce the parent plant but the grandparents. Unless mechanically pollinated, the seed of the hybrid cannot reproduce its own kind. The hybridizing has to be done all over again for each season and every generation.

Way back in the middle of the last century, an Austrian botanist by the name of Gregor Mendel conducted some experiments that demonstrated the basic laws of heredity. Working with peas, Mendel found that if he crossbred green peas with yellow peas, the first generation was all yellow, the second generation was three yellow peas and one green pea. If a smooth pea and a wrinkled pea were crossed, the first generation was all smooth peas, the second generation was three smooth peas and one wrinkled pea.

From all this, Mendel reasoned that the shape of the peas and their coloring was somehow stored within a "memory system" in each pea. As a result of his experiments, Mendel concluded that definite hereditary units, which he called "factors" and which we now call "genes," are responsible for the transmission of certain characteristics from one generation to the next. Also, that each mature organism contains two of each type gene, and when these genes differ, the dominant one is expressed, the recessive remaining dormant. Further, each seed—egg or sperm or botanical seed—contains only one gene of each pair. And the random union of eggs and sperm results in a predictable variety of characteristics in the offspring.

What we now call Mendel's law, because he discovered it, controls the transmission of hereditary factors in all living organisms. His findings explain why a person can be born with the eye coloring of a grandparent instead of his parents.

Mendel's next experiment was to cross smooth yellow peas with wrinkled green peas. The first generation produced smooth yellow peas, demonstrating that smooth and yellow were dominant over wrinkled and green. The second generation produced nine smooth yellow, three smooth green, three wrinkled yellow, and one wrinkled green pea.

You might write it in a series of formulas like this: SY × wg = SwYg. Smooth and yellow being the dominant characteristics, the recessive genes for wrinkled green peas were dormant, present but not making themselves visible. You could see it as the recessive genes being hid in the shadows of their dominant counterparts.

But look at what happened at the next crossing, this one between the grandchildren of the original pair: SwYg × SwYg =

nine smooth yellow peas, three smooth green peas, three wrinkled yellow peas, and one wrinkled green pea. Here's how it
figures out:

wwgg = the wrinkled green pea inherited all recessive
genes, so the recessive trait was expressed, not being over-
shadowed by anything.

YYww, Ygww, gYww = three wrinkled yellow peas. All
have to have a pair of the wrinkled genes, or the wrinkles
couldn't have shown up, but the yellow could have been
produced by any combination of yellow and green, since
yellow is dominant.

SSgg, Swgg, wSgg = three smooth green peas. All have to
have a pair of green genes, because it is a recessive charac-
teristic that can't show up unless no gene carries the dominant color.

Every remaining combination will show up as smooth and
yellow, because each will contain at least one gene that is
smooth and one that is yellow. In their presence, recessive
genes cannot show themselves but must wait, with the possibility of coming to light in the next generation if they are combined with recessive genes like themselves.

Fascinating, eh? My collaborator and her husband have six
children, three of whom are redheads, though neither of the
parents has red hair. How could that happen? Each of the parents carried a dominant gene for brown hair and a recessive
gene for red hair. The recessive genes had expressed themselves in the grandparents' generation with a red-haired aunt
on each side of the family, then had been hidden until the second generation when two recessive genes got together. When

people ask, "Where did they get their red hair?" my friend replies that they got it from aunts on both sides of the family. If she wanted to be technical, she could say, "They got it from the union of two recessive genes."

But we were talking about hybrids, weren't we? Admittedly, improvement within a species can look like evolution—but isn't. The cow, for instance, always remains a cow—a fat cow, a skinny cow, a big cow, a little cow, but still a cow. The cattleman can breed for horns—or no horns; he can breed for a stocky Angus beef-type steer, or big Brown Swiss eyes, or thick Jersey cream, or Holstein running-the-bucket-over abundance; but the result is still a cow, never anything else.

Sometimes people think that the great variety of dogs roaming around in the world is evolution in action and that someday the perfect dog will emerge and then all the low grade specimens will disappear. You'd better not let your own dog catch you thinking out loud, or you'll be in trouble. Again, you can breed for just about any size, shape, color, or disposition of dog that you want. That there are long dogs, short dogs, spindly dogs, scroungy dogs, fluffy dogs, and sleek dogs demonstrates that there is plenty of latitude in the canine gene pool for selective breeding.

There are even dogs that look so much like cats that it's hard for people to tell the difference. But although the cat-looking dogs may fool you, they never fool cats. Cats can tell the difference every time. Nowhere has a half-cat, half-dog specimen ever shown up. There's never been a half-ape, half-man either, no matter what their actions look like. Observation of living creatures and fossil discoveries over the centuries has failed to produce a single shred of proof that anything has ever evolved across the genetic lines.

No new species evolves, merely an improvement of the original species. There's never a crossing over. No mermaids. No centaurs. No dog-cat transitional types. (Horse and donkeys can be crossbred, but the resulting mule is sterile.)

Each species is firmly established by its own extremely complicated genetic coding, and the thing that keeps it that way is the seed.

What is a seed? In the botanical realm, my dictionary explains it like this: "A fertilized mature plant ovule containing an embryo that can form a new plant." A simpler definition of a seed is simply, "a self-contained plant factory."

In the tiny seed lies a mystery that totally baffles the evolutionists, but which the *Manufacturer's Handbook* explains without difficulty.

Just how would you go about starting to "evolve" a self-contained mechanism embodying not only the program capable of reproducing the parent plant, but also containing *life* in a dormant state, just waiting to be released under proper conditions? I wouldn't know how to get started, would you? When you put the question to the learned evolutionists, they're as stumped as we are. But at the beginning of creation, God came up with the seed idea when He said, "Let the earth bring forth grass, the herb yielding seed, and the fruit tree yielding fruit after his kind, whose seed is in itself, upon the earth: and it was so" (Genesis 1:11).

At that time, the "plant factory" principle of the seed was settled, as well as the "after its own kind" principle guaranteeing that every species will remain intact. Can you imagine random happenings over billions of years—evolution's hopeful promise—producing such a complex mechanism as the simple-looking seed? I find it much easier to believe the Bible account, myself.

Maybe you've never thought about the great variation in the design of more than 250,000 varieties of seeds—from the microscopically tiny seed of orchids, each blossom producing millions, to the single forty pounder of certain kinds of tropical palms—each specifically engineered to propagate the parent plant under widely varying environmental conditions.

Every seed contains inside itself a tiny plant, ready to come to life under the proper conditions of moisture, temperature, and atmosphere. Some require low temperatures for germination, while others just sit and do nothing until the ground warms up. Some seeds have to be buried before they can go into action, others—the two-seeded maple seed, for instance—can germinate and reach down into the ground with a taproot without ever touching the soil.

Every seed contains a food supply, a protective covering, and is made of materials readily duplicated in the chemical laboratory with one exception—*life*. The brainiest scientist who ever lived cannot introduce *life* into his mixture of components. That can only be done by Creator God.

Why does a carrot seed produce only a single carrot while a grain of corn produces many grains from a single seed? Evolution shrugs and mumbles "survival of the fittest" or garbles something about mutants. The *Manufacturer's Handbook* says, "God said."

Another great mystery about seeds is why some of them survive for centuries and then produce a living plant while others last only a few years. At the Kenilworth Aquatic Gardens in Washington, D.C., is a family of lotus plants grown from seeds which had laid dormant in a dried-up lake bed in China for a thousand years. Grain stored for centuries in the Egyptian pyramids produced a crop when it was planted.

How about the variety of seed coverings—from the extremely hard shells of the palm seed to the cottony milkweed and the plasticlike shells of corn, wheat, rice, and other grains? Each type of covering is exactly suited to the conditions under which it must respond to the words of the Creator who issued the command to be fruitful and multiply and replenish the earth. Each seed is equipped with everything it needs to do its part in fulfilling that assignment.

Look at the complexities of the transportation process for the widespread distribution of plant species. I call it the Heavenly Travel Bureau, involving birds, wind, water, and animals—including people.

Birds are probably nature's best-known seed carriers. When folks wash the family jalopy of bird droppings loaded with seeds, the water drains off into the yard. Next spring you might see there a new kind of weed you'd never seen before. Guess where it came from—air mail. During berry season, my car is often colorfully decorated by bird droppings containing the seeds of berries I painstakingly nurtured but never got to eat because the robins got there first. Some seeds are digested inside the bird, of course, but plenty survive to multiply and replenish the earth.

The wind is the heavenly travel agent carrying many seeds whose perfect design for air travel is way ahead of human knowledge of aerodynamics. The seeds of the Zanonia in the jungles of Java can glide a quarter of a mile. Gliders as well as swept-back wing aircraft have come from the study of this structure. The tissue-paper-thin butterfly-type wings of the seed, about six inches across, carry 1/100 of a pound per square foot. The relationship of the unique wing design to the center of gravity deflects the wing tip upward, providing a stability in fight—without fins—that our best aeronautical engineers have not been able to duplicate.

Every spring I am faced with rain gutters clogged with airborne maple, elm, and ash tree offspring requiring prompt attention if I don't want them to germinate and grow trees on my roof. We've all seen children blow the fluff of a gone-to-seed dandelion blossom, sending hundreds of little seed parachutes dancing their way to a neighbor's lawn.

Other seeds are borne by the wind along the ground. I have seen the tumbleweeds of Texas so densely packed they actually pushed over strong fences as the wind got behind them. Once, a monster roll of tumbleweed threatened to push my car off the highway in a gale-force wind.

Many plants literally shoot their seeds into flight. Have you ever poked your finger at a touch-me-not along the roadside and seen it shoot out seeds like a small gun? Violets have pods containing seeds which are shot several feet when the pod shrinks through drying in the warm spring air.

Some seeds hitchhike on whatever inadvertently offers them a ride. Growing up in the Connecticut countryside, I spent a lot of time picking cockleburs off me and my dog. What did I do with them when I had picked them off? Why, I just dropped them to the ground, of course, unwittingly fulfilling another step in the distribution of those prickly seed carriers over many miles of countryside. Beggar-ticks, Spanish needles, pitchforks, and sandburs are a few other hitchhiking seeds.

Some seeds are carried with deliberate intention on the part of the carrier. Johnny Appleseed may be the best known of these carriers. 'Way back in 1806 he started down the Ohio River with two canoes filled with apple seeds. Every time he saw a likely spot for an apple orchard, he stopped and planted apple seeds. For forty years he planted apple orchards and gave the early settlers the benefit of his experience in apple-tree husbandry.

Can evolution account for the unending variety of fruit, the seed of each doing its particular "thing" with unfailing precision? Years ago when I was an inquisitive student in a botany class, one of the students asked the professor, "Sir, do you be-

lieve that evolution can account for all these varieties of plant
life?"

The professor's reply was to the point: "I hope I'm not trying
to teach a class of idiots who could believe in such fairy tales.
Let the evidence speak for itself." And so it does.

"But aren't the cells of all living things similar in design, and
doesn't that prove that everything evolved from a single parent
cell?" old diehard is still arguing.

"No more than the fact that Williamsburg buildings being
made of brick means that they all evolved from the same
building," I say. What the cellular construction of living things
means is that in His infinite wisdom, the Creator God who designed this whole system found it good to invent and use the
cell as the basic building block for all living organisms.

In my profession, we have a saying: "If a thing works, don't
fix it."

Although the cell structure appears in all plant and animal
life forms, the cells themselves are vastly different from one
another. Look at what happens when you cut your finger. If all
cells in all living organisms behaved in the same manner, the
new parts manufactured by your body to repair the damaged
finger structure might turn out to be bird feathers instead of
human skin, or fingernail tissue instead of flesh. But that never
happens. The Creator God has programmed every cell to exactly replicate itself when necessary. Whenever a body part is
damaged, adjacent cells go immediately to work to replace the
injured parts, starting deep inside the wound and working out-
ward to the surface in a faithful duplication of parts so that the
repair job is sometimes hardly detectable.

To me, this is one of the marvels of God's programming
skill, that each cell is equipped with perfect wisdom to know
exactly how to replace the structure in which it is contained
and never to meddle in the business of other cells.

When God said that everything should bring forth fruit after its own kind, He made it impossible for anything else to happen. To this day, every seed, every cell, does its own thing, century after century, with unerring precision.

While all cells follow a similar design, there is a fundamental difference between plant and animal cells. Plant cells contain the green pigment chlorophyll, which enables the plant to combine the sun's energy with carbon dioxide and water vapor to make sugar for themselves and oxygen for us. Plants use what we throw away—our CO_2 lung garbage—and give back what we need for sustaining life—oxygen. All this is peculiar to the plant kingdom and never takes place in the animal kingdom. Instead of transforming the sun's energy directly into food, the animal kingdom feeds on the high energy source stored in plants and takes it directly into the digestive system.

If all this complexity evolved from the single cell of a common ancestor, there ought to be at least one dog somewhere who makes his own dog food, using the leaves sprouting from his forehead. Or there ought to be at least one cow who doesn't eat grass and chew her cud but uses her own bright green, chlorophyll-laden fronds girdling her midsection to make a mountain of "sun sugar" fodder without ever having to nibble a single clover blossom.

Which way is all the evidence pointing so far? Does it suggest a series of accidental happenings which add up to all this beautifully functioning genetic coding within your cells? Not to me, it doesn't. My own faith leads me to believe that an all-wise Creator is responsible, not only for designing the whole system and whirling it into operation, but even today sustaining it all ". . . by the word of his power . . ." (Hebrews 1:3).

"But doesn't environment ever have any bearing on these things?" our squawker interrupts again.

That was a subject much debated in college when I was a

student. The way they phrased it then, in debate after debate, was: "Which has the greatest effect on living things—environment or heredity?" Leaving a Creator God out of the equation, as folks had a tendency to do in those days, no one ever came up with a conclusive answer. But I have observed that while organisms may develop certain behavioral characteristics as they respond to environmental conditions, these characteristics are not passed on to the next generation, such transmissions being limited to hereditary characteristics. Of course, there are always so-called scientists around who say they have proven what a botanist named Jean Baptiste Lamarck claimed to have proven more than fifty years before Darwin got into the act. Lamarck claimed that acquired characteristics *can* be transmitted genetically to offspring—that a giraffe can increase the length of its neck by reaching for the highest leaves and that his offspring would have longer necks as a result. I haven't seen anything like that happening to anyone I know, have you? That Lamarck died penniless and blind, with his "research" condemned by the French Academy of Sciences, hasn't kept other people from heading down the same blind alley.

Some honor his disgrace even in the light of August Weismann's discovery that changes in body cells—*including gene mutations*—are never passed on to the sperm or egg cells. One such misguided fellow was the Austrian biologist, Paul Kammerer, who claimed to have demonstrated the transmission of acquired characteristics. How did he end up? According to the August, 1981, issue of *Discover* magazine, after he was accused of fraud, he wrote a note of denial and committed suicide. But even that was not enough for some people who keep trying to prove something that can never be proven—because it doesn't square with Creator God's account.

Considering all the intricately interrelated complexities of life in the world around us, I cannot help but believe that a Creator God did it all.

And *now* back to Brother Adam.

9

Man Blows It

Adam had it made. He was created in the very image of God by God Himself and placed in the Garden of Eden—perfect plan, perfect workmanship, perfect environment. He even had a perfect wife, tailor-made to suit him exactly. God formed her from one of Adam's ribs, which He took from Adam's body one day while Adam was sleeping. When he woke up and saw her, Adam must have thought he was dreaming. But he wasn't. She was real!

"Eve," he sighed, "you're the only woman in the world for me!" And he was right.

Now, Adam could have eaten of the tree of life and he would have lived forever. Life in a beautiful garden, no parking problems, a luscious wife, no competition, plenty to eat, no income taxes, no laundry bills, no rowdy neighbors or PTA meetings. Why, he even had fellowship with *God* on a first-hand, personal basis. The Bible says that Adam and God walked together in the cool of the evening. That's close fellowship. Nothing in between them—no shadows, no coverups, no

Watergates, no guilt, no sins. Just perfect innocence and freedom.

Can you imagine goofing an idyllic situation like that? Well Adam did, but good.

God had told Adam he could eat of the fruit of every tree in the garden except one, the tree of the knowledge of good and evil. That one was off limits. If he ate of it, God said, he would surely die. If he didn't eat of it, all systems would be go—forever.

Before he even got as far as the tree of life, Adam rebelled. He just had to sample that forbidden fruit of the tree of the knowledge of good and evil. Satan, the snake, told Adam's wife, Eve, that if she would eat of that tree, she would be as God, knowing good and evil, and that naturally whetted her appetite. (Up to then, there had been no evil. It was nonexistent. God had pronounced His creation to be very good.)

Her curiosity aroused, Eve didn't resist temptation, she succumbed to it. She ate of the forbidden fruit, and she gave Adam a bite, too.

It'll happen every time. A no-no just naturally creates an appetite in us. If you don't believe it, put a kid in a room with a basketful of beautiful apples and one little old wormy apple. Tell the kid he can eat the whole basket of good apples if he wants to, but that he's not to touch the wormy apple. Then go out of the room for five minutes. When you come back, the beautiful fruit will be there, untouched. And there will be just half a worm inside the wormy apple. The other half will be in the kid. That's our nature.

Adam and Eve ate the forbidden fruit because they wanted to be as God.

God said, "If you eat, it'll kill you," but what God said was beside the point.

A snake said, "Oh, come now. Surely you don't think God would kill off His favorite creation—mankind? Of course not." His voice was smooth as oil, *so* persuasive. And Adam and Eve weren't wary. They didn't know yet that whenever you begin to reason together, looking to your head for answers instead of to God, you're headed for big trouble. You've had it.

The devil is always a deceitful operator. In real life, he doesn't wear his costume like he does in melodramas. In real life, he never comes on strong in long red underwear and a forked tail, twirling a black moustache. He comes softly, as a smoothie, an angel of light, a beautiful serpent—there's no telling what his disguise might be. And he always begins by casting doubt on the truth and trustworthiness of the Word of God. He always wants to dilute it, to water it down with reasonableness.

Why does the human mind listen to snake talk in preference to God talk? Because, according to Isaiah 1:5, the whole head is sick. Did you think half of your head was dependable? Think again. Not a hair on it, nor anything under the hair, is reliable. It isn't now, it wasn't then. Actually, about the only useful function the head performs—until your mind is regenerated and reprogrammed by God's Holy Spirit——is to keep your ears from flapping together. Our carnal minds have to be renewed and renewed and renewed until we have the very mind of Christ in us. Until that takes place, the less you rely on your mind, the better off you'll be.

Our minds were blown in the Garden of Eden. You don't have to take acid to blow your mind. A blown mind is standard equipment when you're born.

Man's first sin was to trust his own mind instead of trusting the God who made it. The King James translation of the *Manufacturer's Handbook* didn't come out until 1611, and so Adam hadn't read Proverbs 3:5, 6 where it says ". . . lean not unto thine own understanding. In all thy ways acknowledge him, and he shall direct thy paths." But it wasn't ignorance of God's will that tripped Adam, it was willfulness, wanting to do his own thing. And he did it.

Immediately, death and decay were set in motion for all his posterity, including us. Adam's first child was a murderer. God cursed the ground, and said, "You'll have to contend with it unless you want to starve to death." Right away, there began to be mutations in the plant kingdom.

Both chemicals and nuclear radiation can cause mutations, which are tortured reprogrammings of the cells of a plant or an animal. We automatically receive some nuclear radiation. When solar rays come from the sun and hit our outer atmosphere, they break down into scatter radiation which we call neutrons. In about thirteen minutes, these neutrons break down into protons and electrons—unless they combine with some other group to make an element. In the process, they are emitting radiation, causing life to diminish, to be destroyed.

You can take a radish seed, which is smooth and regular and produces a well-organized leaf and plant, and expose it to nuclear radiation. Afterward, you can plant it, and what will come up? The ugliest, thorniest thistle you ever saw. If you know somebody who has a nuclear reactor, who will let you take your seeds and put them in it before you plant them, you can raise a garden full of hideous mutants.

That there were mutations in the plant kingdom after Adam's fall is clear from Genesis 3:17, 18 which says, "And to Adam, God said, 'Because you listened to your wife and ate the fruit when I told you not to, I have placed a curse upon the soil. All your life you will struggle to extract a living from it. It will grow thorns and thistles for you. . .' " (TLB). Adam hadn't seen any thorns and thistles before he sinned. There weren't any then. But we've had a more than adequate supply of them ever since.

Not only did the plant kingdom take a turn for the worse when Adam sinned, but the animal kingdom became enemies of people. Everything took a nose dive because of original sin, which is another name for Adam's goof.

Not long after Adam came down with original sin, everybody else caught it, and things got so bad that God was sorry He had made man in the first place (*see* Genesis 6:6). Why, man was so wicked, the Bible says, that the thoughts of his heart were only evil continually (*see* Genesis 6:5). About 1,600 years from the beginning of things, God made up His mind He'd have to start the whole thing over again from scratch, because the old mess wasn't worth patching up.

But there was still one man who had stayed in touch with Him, and so God gave that man an assignment.

"Noah," He said, "it's going to rain. And there's going to be a flood. I want you to build an ark." He gave him very specific directions, better than a blueprint, about what he should make it from, and just what the dimensions were to be. "This will be the ark of deliverance," He said. "Whoever goes aboard will be saved; whoever doesn't will drown." There was no in-between, no second chance.

This was heavy stuff for Noah, because there were no words in his vocabulary for *rain* or *flood*. The weather had been perfect up to then, and everything got watered by a mist that rose up from the ground (Genesis 2:6). They hadn't even invented umbrellas yet. Noah certainly didn't need a boat to get around on dry land, and he didn't know what God was talking about. But he figured God did, and that was good enough for him. He started to work.

Can you imagine what the neighbors thought when they

heard him hammering and came over to stand on the sidewalk and superintend the job?

"Brother Noah, what's that big old thing parked out in your driveway?"

"That's an ark."

"An ark? What's that?"

"Well, it's a kind of a boat—like a floodmobile—for safety from the flood."

"The flood. What's that?"

"I don't know, exactly, but God said He was going to send one. It'll be made out of rain."

"Rain? What's that?"

They were dealing in absolute unknowns, but Noah knew God and trusted Him. And when it came time to go aboard the ark, the animals didn't argue. The unclean animals came two by two and the clean ones came seven by seven and marched up the gangplank, waving good-bye to their relatives who stayed behind.

Now, if evolution had been true, there'd been no need to go to all the trouble to save two of everything. God could have wiped the whole world out and let it start up again all by itself.

One day when I was reading the Book of Genesis, refreshing my memory about how all these things happened, I got to wondering about the ark and insects. The *Manufacturer's Handbook* made it plain that wild animals, livestock, and birds were invited to enter the ark, and mention was made of the creatures that move along the ground, as well as food for everybody. But what about the insects that didn't exactly fit the classification of creatures that move along the ground or fly through the air?

I had barely acknowledged the question in my mind when the answer appeared alongside it in the form of a trio of other questions. "Did you ever see a camel without fleas? A honeysuckle blossom without a honeybee or two? (Noah would have put on board a good supply of blossoms to keep the humming-birds fed, wouldn't he?) Or a bale of hay that didn't have at least one spider web?" I decided the bug world wasn't left out after all. It's like ants at a picnic. You don't have to invite them. They come automatically.

But the human race was too intelligent to join the parade. They used their common sense and criticized.

"You mean this kooky old preacher Noah thinks he knows more than Professor Tinkling Cymbal down at our Sanhedrinite Theological Cemetery? Why, he and Dr. Sounding Brass have just coauthored a paper in which they prove that God couldn't possibly destroy His favorite creation."

"Forget it, brother. Everybody knows that Noah's an old kook."

Can you imagine how they ridiculed Noah? A man listening to God is always out of step with the world. He doesn't mind it, but the world usually does.

And so they backed off, staying away in droves. Only eight people ended up in the ark with all the animals: Noah, his wife, their three sons and their wives. Only eight people out of the whole human race were stupid enough to listen to God in the face of all the learned evidence to the contrary. Those eight were saved. The rest gurgled under the flood and were seen no more, except as fossils.

When the waters receded, the human population of the world was eight people, all saved from the flood by God's special provision. But instead of keeping the world all newly washed and clean, man quickly turned to his own ways again, and became more evil than ever. Even Noah got drunk.

After he'd been cooped up all that time in a covered-up canoe with his wife, sons, daughters-in-law, and a boatload of hyenas howling at hight, roosters crowing at the crack of dawn, and ostriches racing the horses to get exercise, he probably felt

entitled to a little nip. I mean, the man had an awesome re-
sponsibility on his shoulders. How would you like to be head
of an expedition to start the whole world over again?

Later, God sent fire and brimstone on Sodom and Gomor-
rah. Perhaps the only reason why He didn't wipe out all of
creation again with another flood was that He kept seeing
rainbows—and they reminded Him of His promise to Noah
that He'd never send another flood to destroy the world.

In the beginning, man didn't look like a hairless ape—he
looked like God. And he didn't act like a hairless ape—until he
decided to disobey God and eat of the forbidden fruit. Disobe-
dience and rebellion made a monkey out of him, and from that
day, he began to deteriorate from the glory in which God had
created him. The "facts" of evolution are exactly backward
from what really happened.

The first man, instead of being a mutant, a freak ape who
would have died out in a couple of generations, was so full of
life he hung around the earth for nine hundred thirty years—
even though he ate a deadly poison when he was still a young
man. But from then until now, the natural life span of man has
diminished.

In the very beginning, the vapor barrier around the world
filtered out the nuclear radiation from the sun. But when God
let the vapor barrier fall as part of the water that flooded the
earth, the filter was broken, and the radiation reaching us increased. And as the nuclear radiation increased, our life span
diminished. Things went from good to bad and from bad to
worse because man made the wrong choice.

My good friend and fellow engineer V. L. Westberg of Son-
oma, California, has sent me some interesting observations
about the creation and the flood that are worth sharing here.
To begin with, Westberg told me, when God divided the waters below the sky (*firmament,* if you're reading in the King

James Version) from the waters above the sky, He was setting things up to serve a purpose that was not yet apparent.

What was the form of the waters above the sky? Geologists believe they were like an ice canopy that totally surrounded the earth and acted as a barrier against the bombardment of high-intensity solar energy. This ice-crystal greenhouse helped to retain the heat of the earth's inner core, maintaining a worldwide tropical climate while at the same time funneling to us energy from the sun, properly attuned to the needs of the earth's vegetation.

Not only is there evidence that such a canopy was formed at the time of earth's creation about ten thousand years ago, but similar ice-ring formations on other heavenly bodies have been discovered in pictures taken by fly-by explorer satellites.

Because of the extremely low temperatures and the condition of weightlessness in outer space, the waters above the sky could not exist in vapor form. That accounts for the ice spears interlocked into a perfect canopy, so that as the Bible account says, it had never rained on earth before the flood.

Now, assuming that rain falls at the rate of about twenty miles per hour, when Noah was told that it would begin to arrive at the earth's surface in seven days (Genesis 7:4), that *could* mean that the ice canopy was in the neighborhood of three thousand miles above the earth. As the earth tilted on its axis, ice began melting at the equator and continued to fall as rain for forty days and forty nights, until the whole earth was covered.

Eventually, as the center of the great ice canopy melted, the portions over the north and south poles, being farthest away from the sun, and thus remaining intact, would have lost their centrifugal force and finally landed with a mighty crash, forming the polar ice caps still in evidence.

Their fall to earth would have been somewhat cushioned by

the warm air trapped beneath them, which would have been displaced in a mighty "swoosh," which could even be the sudden wind referred to in Genesis 8:1. That could also explain the geologists' finding of mammoth fossils six hundred feet down on the continental shelf, indicating that water to a depth of four hundred fifty feet was added above the normal level.

The sudden deep-freeze conditions when the remains of the ice canopy collapsed on the poles could account for the fact that dinosaurs, mammoths, and other large animals have been discovered intact below the ice cap, frozen in an upright position with vegetation still in their teeth, just as if they had been caught completely unaware by a sudden and unexpected cataclysmic happening. Huge coal fields have also been discovered below the ice caps. Bare mountain peaks and mud-filled valleys with redwood trees buried deeply where the cold prevents their present growth are another indication of a drastic climatic change in the past.

Further evidence of the possibility of such a happening is the presence of polar ice caps just beneath the surface of the Arctic sea, and the presence of ice caves filled with canopy slush at latitudes 42–47°.

As that first rain penetrated fissures in the earth's crust, tremendous steam pressures began to lift the hills into mountains, a geological phenomenon which continues to this day. The lifting formed large lakes whose drainages washed great gullies such as the Grand Canyon when debris dams began to collapse. No such canyons have been found under the ice caps, which could indicate that those areas were flash frozen, escaping the ravages of receding floodwaters.

With the appearance of direct, unfiltered sunlight for the first time after the canopy had melted and the flood ended, the first rainbow appeared. It all ties together to say that there might be something to the Bible account after all.

Thanks, Brother Westberg, for this fascinating rundown of scientific Bible truth.

I have some evidence of some of these strange world-changing events in my own house. Let me tell you about it.

On a recent trip to the vicinity of Worland, Wyoming, I came across some perfectly formed fish fossils, imprints in a sandstone formation about a mile above sea level. Some were an inch long, others several inches from end to end, but all were perfectly clear imprints of what had been real, living, swimming fish until something happened to stop them. Whatever it was must have set in quite suddenly, because it encased them in sand, which solidified into a perfectly sealed burial ground that preserved them from decay for many years.

How did all those fish get to the top of a mountain thousands of feet above sea level? "Flying fish?" someone answers. But flying fish have never been able to soar more than a few feet above their watery home. How could they have blasted off to such a great height—as if they had suddenly evolved into rocket ships?

And if they did fly that high, why didn't they fly back the way they came, downhill this time? But there is no ocean water within many miles of Worland, Wyoming. It's all semiarid country, with lots of sand, dust, rocks, and armadillos, not even a small pond for the fish to have come from. Still, there they were, thousands of them, big and little, all encased in their sandstone coffins.

The only thing I can think of that could account for fish fossils in such a location is the flood. When the rains came and the waters rose above the tops of the highest mountains, the fish all rose with it. All the fish were above the mountaintops, getting along swimmingly until the flood waters began to recede. As the great pressure on the earth's crust began to distort the mantle rock—the outer skin of our planet—great turbulence resulted, sloshing zillions of tons of water around, and causing fish, sand, rocks, mud, and everything else to be churned together into one great soupy mess.

As things began to dry out, fish that were caught in the swirling sand became encased in that semiliquid mass of material. As the weight of it all compressed the sand into a solid state, those living fish were instantly changed into dead ones, so perfectly preserved that you can even see the imprint of their fins, gills, eyes, and other fish parts perfectly.

But you don't need my Wyoming fossil fish to convince you that the flood really happened. Hear this from Dick Eastman's *University of the World* (Ventura, Calif.: Regal Books, 1983, pp. 26, 27):

> According to the science of ethnology ... if the Bible record of a great flood is true, we should read about such a flood in the ancient writings of numerous of the various thirty-three races of people for which records are available. Evaluating such records is rather revealing.
>
> 1. First, we note that of the thirty-three races examined, all thirty-three, even though widely located and separated, clearly mention some type of flood, either total or partial, that happened at approximately the time of the biblical flood. Thus 100 percent have a record of the flood in their archives. This cannot be a coincidence.
> 2. Second, thirty-one of these races include in their records specific reference to the flood being totally destructive, exactly as the Bible describes. Thus, 94 percent of these races have in their ancient tradition and beliefs a record of a complete flood.
> 3. Third, thirty-two, or 97 percent, state in their traditions that man was miraculously rescued from the

flood. Of this group, twenty-eight declare salvation came by boat or ark. Thus, 85 percent express belief in an ark.

4. Fourth, thirty races, 91 percent, relate in their traditions that animals also were miraculously saved, thus protecting their species.

5. Fifth, twenty-five, or 76 percent, include as part of their ancient records information about the ark landing on a mountain after the waters receded.

6. Sixth, twenty-nine, or 88 percent, describe birds being sent forth from the vessel to test whether the flood waters were receding.

7. Seventh, thirty of the thirty-three races, or 91 percent, mention some sort of divine favor being shown toward those who were saved, in particular by a "bow" of colors in the sky.

8. Finally, thirty-one, or 94 percent, speak of worship toward a deity being offered by those who were saved after the destructive flood.

The evidence . . . appears both obvious and overwhelming. There is a God who has communicated His love to mankind . . . through His written Word, the Bible, and through His Living Word, Jesus Christ, His Son.

Amen, Brother Eastman, amen. All that's pretty persuasive, isn't it? And there's no need for me to remind anyone that sightings of remnants of Noah's Ark on top of Mount Ararat are becoming more frequent with every passing year. Why, the next thing you know, someone will have found an ancient scroll with the notations Noah made when God gave him the exact verbal blueprints, 'way back in the sixth chapter of Genesis.

Did Noah's flood really happen? Considering the evidence

in line with God's own Word on the subject, I have to say yes.

Fascinating, eh? And just in case you have a tendency to blame Adam for blowing it, hear this:

Given a choice between obedience to God and doing his own thing, man would still choose the wrong way. We are still capable of goofing it—that talent has never left us.

Without God, every atom in all creation has been in torment ever since God put a curse on His creation. Nothing is settled in itself, nothing is satisfied with anything outside itself—until Jesus comes to give peace.

Is this some nonsensical religious notion? No, it is an established fact.

The Law of Repulsion is built right into the core of every atom in existence. Any physicist—pagan or believer in God—will tell you that the core of the atom is totally disturbed, unhappy, striving to grab onto something to obtain completeness—or to give up something in order to be a whole something instead of one plus an extra piece of leftover tagging along. Scientists even have a name for it—Coulomb's Law of Mutual Repulsion.

What holds atoms together then? Why don't we have atomic blasts going on all the time without our having to go to a lot of trouble to unglue the atom to release the explosive energy that's inside?

That's an interesting question.

If you ask a pagan scientist, "What holds atoms together?" he'll clear his throat and say, "Well, er, ah—there's an, er, ah—force that holds atoms together. We call it 'binding power.' "

If you ask him what the binding power is, he'll look at his digital computer wristwatch and tell you he's sorry, but he's about to be late for another appointment. You can't blame him for that. It's bound to be embarrassing to be reminded that you really have no answer. Especially when it's true.

No pagan scientist alive can tell you what this essential binding power is that keeps atoms from blowing up in our faces continually. But they're probably thankful there *is* such a thing.

The apostle Paul knew what it was—because God had told him all about it. When he was writing to the church at Colossae, he told them that Jesus is the visible representation of the invisible God, that in Him all things were created, that all things exist through Him and in and for Him, and that ". . . in Him all things consist—cohere, *are held together*" (Colossians 1:17 AMP, *italics mine*).

In Him you are complete, whole. Without Him, you are incomplete, fractional, always looking for something but programmed for repulsion by everything you meet.

The nuclei of your atoms contain an assortment of miserable particles, protons and neutrons clustered into a group. They hate one another. They repel one another. They're trying their best to blow up, to get away from one another.

In physics, it's called randomness. The atoms in a piece of metal that look solid are in a state of torment wandering around in that metallic structure in random fashion, seeking for completeness, seeking to take on something or to give up something. That's due to the curse that God placed on the whole creation when His chosen people, mankind, chose to disobey God and do their own thing. That's how deeply original sin reads out in every one of your atoms. The nucleus of every one of them is in the same state of torment or randomness.

We cannot overcome this torment in physics. We can't overcome it in metallurgy. An airplane wing drops off without any warning. A bridge collapses suddenly, because the atoms cannot tolerate one another, and they get divorced, going into what's called a "slip plane" within the crystal structure. We make bridges stronger than they need to be to compensate for this possibility, and we do all sorts of things to metal to try to overcome this inherent defect. We call it stress relieving.

But the human personality is never stress relieved until Jesus moves in and brings peace into the center of every atom of our being. He's the only one who can bring us into the solid state, where all parts work together in harmony toward a common goal—good for all concerned. Without Him, we're in an amorphous, uncrystallized state, like window glass, ready to shatter into a million pieces, cutting everything within reach, if someone fails to handle us with kid gloves.

**Edsel Murphy Egghead Analog:
Solid State—Mistaking a tubful of fast-settling epoxy cement for bubblebath.**

Talk about touchy! That's us—without Jesus.

The wages of sin—what we get into when we fall short of the best God has planned for us—is death. Every man has inherited the fruit of Adam's rebellion, and death is still its consequence. Men die. As a matter of fact, they are born dead, and remain in corpsehood all their lives unless they are born again of the Spirit of God. Then they will live forever, enjoying eternal life.

You can never rest quietly until you know Jesus. You've got to have all kinds of things going on. Entertainment—a boob tube for each eyeball. Noise—walk down the street with a blasting transistor radio for each ear. Something to do with your mouth, something to do with your hands. No balance, no equilibrium. No nothing—except misery—until you enter God's rest, the rest promised to those who believe in Him, who trust Him, who come to Him (Hebrews 4 or Matthew 11:28, take your pick). He asks, "Wilt thou be made whole?" (John 5:6), and if we tell Him yes, He makes us complete in Him (*see* Colossians 2:10).

In God's rest, all forces are balanced out; there is no struggle. Jesus says, "Be perfect." That means, "Be complete, be whole," and there's no way to do it without Him. He is the Rock, and He makes us *solid*.

"Mine iniquities are gone over my head," David said (*see* Psalms 38:4), when he was overwhelmed by fear, anxiety, worry about the mistakes he had made. They were some dillies, but Jesus cleaned him up so thoroughly that later God could say that David was "a man after my own heart" (*see* Acts 13:22). Before I met Jesus, my iniquities had gone over my head, too. On those rare occasions when I had nothing to worry about, I worried about that. It was too good to last. Something bad was bound to happen.

Edsel Murphy Egghead Analog:
Orbital   Mechanics—Psychiatrists   without
Jesus. They go around in circles.

I couldn't enjoy the relatively good times for worrying about what would happen when they were taken away. No question about it, I wasn't much better off than a dead man. In fact, I *was* a dead man. But I wasn't alone. I had lots of company. Almost everybody around me was dead, too.

Death doesn't take away physical life, you know. Death is simply what's left over after life has departed. A century ago, man's life expectancy was only about thirty years. Today we've boosted it to seventy, keeping the corpses quivering forty years longer by cramming all kinds of chemicals into their veins. But chemically induced quivering is a long way off from born-again vitality. Being propped up by pills, ointments, and tranquilizers can't touch real living.

Compare our seventy years—with additives—with the nine-hundred-and-some years Adam stuck around after he took poison into his system. His spiritual death took place when he took the first bite of the forbidden fruit. But it took almost ten centuries for the enormous vitality that God placed in the human race in the beginning to die out of Adam's physical body. Today, we've reached the point where we can't build nursing homes fast enough to accommodate the corpses who are still breathing.

No wonder some folks are talking about euthanasia. And the thing is, the picture would keep on getting bleaker and bleaker—except that God has a plan. Let's look at that next.

10

Can Man Be Recycled?

The condition of fallen man looks pretty hopeless, doesn't it? The apostle Paul cried out, "O wretched man that I am! who shall deliver me from the body of this death?" (Romans 7:24). Sometimes it looks as if we'll just keep on going down the sliding board until there's nothing left of us except our blisters. Then they'll burst, and we'll be gone. Annihilated. Nothing left.

In the natural, according to the Second Law of Thermodynamics, that's what would happen to us, all right. But because God understood exactly how it would go unless He intervened, He intervened. He built a remedy for sin and death right into the system. He made a way for us to live, after all, not just to hang around for thirty years or seventy years, or even for nine hundred and thirty years. He made a way for us to live forever, just as we could have done if Adam and Eve hadn't taken things into their own hands and applied their own rotten reasonableness to what God had said.

The way to live forever doesn't begin with patching up what we are now with chemical additives or crutches or false teeth, wigs, or replacement hip sockets. The way to eternal life begins with a new beginning. We have to start over, to be born again. We have to die to ourselves in a flood of water baptism and rise to newness of life in Jesus.

**Hillism:
Under His wings, fetters become feathers.**

This second birth is not a physical rebirth but a spiritual one. And it happens when we trust Jesus to save us from all that we are and all that Adam was. Dying on the cross, Jesus paid the penalty for all our turning away from God and made us holy in His sight.

And how do we get this gift that God provided through Jesus because He loved us too much to let us perish in our own way?

Simply by accepting it.

"Is that all?" someone squeaks.

"Yes, that's all."

"But how do you know, Mr. Hill?"

"Because it happened to me."

I tried life my own way for forty-eight years, and I didn't like the outcome. I was successful, but tormented, an empty, miserable, striving, struggling, dreary, drab corpse, trying to live it up. What a drag! A graveyard dweller trying to do his thing in a cemetery ghoulish with dead things. The law of sin and death had set in for me—but good.

I met Jesus shortly thereafter, and now, crowding eighty, I'm closer to thirty than I was at twenty-nine, because I'm hooked up with the Head Man of the universe, the One who made it all in the first place. I have in me the vital energy of God that He intended from the beginning to be the life of His people. But we blew it when we took our own way of darkness, worshiping our Educated Idiot Box, that calcium deposit on the top eight inches of our skeleton, instead of worshiping God and following His way of light.

Jesus' blood is the antidote for the deadly poison of our rebellion. And it doesn't work by any gradual, evolutionary process. The truth is, none of us needs changing, we need wiping out. We need to start all over, be born again, and become new creatures with no hangover from the past. And it just happens that that's exactly what He promises to do for us when we turn to Him.

"Therefore if any man be in Christ, he is a new creature: old things are passed away; behold, all things are become new" (2 Corinthians 5:17).

"And you, who were dead in trespasses and the uncircumcision of your flesh, God made alive together with him, having forgiven us all our trespasses" (Colossians 2:13 RSV). Isn't that good news?

From death to life in one fell swoop is a whole lot better than gradual change, isn't it? Gradually, the dead decompose. Resurrection has to be all of a sudden. And I'm in favor of resurrection, aren't you?

There's nothing unscientific about resurrection. We see it all the time in nature. A grain of wheat falls into the ground and dies, the winter snow covers it, and then all at once it's spring. The dead grain springs up into a new stalk, and before long, its ears are heavy with kernels of grain.

How does a person go about being resurrected, raised from the dead, born again to start all over as a brand-new creature so alive that he will live forever?

The formula is so simple that the world refuses to believe it. They'd rather stay dead than to do something as uncomplicated as following the directions in the *Manufacturer's Hand-*

book. They're there, plain as day, steps 1, 2, 3.

In the Book of Romans (10:9), Paul wrote, under the inspiration of the Holy Spirit of God:

1. If you confess with your lips that Jesus is Lord
2. And believe in your heart that God raised Him from the dead
3. You will be saved.

Easy as 1, 2, 3, isn't it? Just say, "Jesus is my Lord," and believe in your heart that God raised Him from the dead, and you are automatically saved from death and from a whole lot of other second-best things. You enter into the new creaturehood of 2 Corinthians 5:17, and that includes eternal life. The whole works that the *Manufacturer's Handbook* promises in John 3:16:

For God so loved the world, that he gave his only begotten Son, that whosoever believeth in him should not perish, but have everlasting life.

For my money, that sure beats evolving from dead to decomposed.

**Hillism:
Life without Jesus will end
in alcohol, pills, or windowsills.**

11

Where Do We Go From Here?

Once we have been resurrected, raised from our own deadness by accepting the brand-new life Jesus came to bring us, then what?

The first thing to realize is that Jesus' gift of new creaturehood is not like gifts the world gives you. They ring your doorbell, make the delivery, and take off, leaving you on your own as far as using the gift is concerned. But Jesus doesn't give you new creaturehood, wave good-bye, and take off. He sticks right there with you, living His life through you. Where the things of God are concerned, the Giver comes with the gift—and stays forever. "I'm the way," He says, "and I'll never leave you or forsake you."

Pretty good bargain, isn't it? A perfect new life with built-in maintenance in exchange for an old life that was ready for the graveyard. "Something for nothing," is the way it's often explained.

As we learn progressively to yield to His new life in us,

things get better and better. Colossians 2:10 says that you are complete in Him. There's nothing lacking in your life when you're complete in Jesus. If that once gets hold of your gizzard, you'll never have to struggle for anything again. But if it doesn't—if you let doubt and unbelief grip your gizzard instead, you'll fight a losing battle all the way and miss out on the best God has for you. You'll be a billy-goat Christian, always saying, "Yes, but—"

When God had led the children of Israel out of slavery in Egypt to freedom in the land He had promised them, they could have just walked into the land and taken it over. No sweat. But they refused to take His word for it that the victory would be theirs. He said He'd make all the arrangements for them. He'd proved Himself to them time and time again in effecting their deliverance, but their gizzards were still full of unbelief, full of trusting themselves instead of trusting God.

"We must be very careful, brethren," they said. "We'd better send some spies in and check this thing out. Maybe God doesn't know what we're up against."

And so they formed a church committee to judge the Word of God, to see whether or not God knew what He was talking about. And that's where the trouble started. A church committee is a good thing when it minds its own business. But when it sets out to snoop into God's business, to see if God is telling the truth or maybe pulling a fast one, that same committee is a dreadful thing. It judges by common sense, and common sense comes from a sick head, so it naturally comes up with sick answers.

The committee sent spies into the Promised Land. There they saw giants so large they made the spies look—and feel— like grasshoppers. But two of the spies, Joshua and Caleb, saw things that impressed them even more than the giants did. They saw a beautiful land flowing with milk and honey, a land so fertile that it took two men just to carry a single bunch of grapes!

The other spies were more impressed with the giants than with the grapes. But Joshua and Caleb said, "Aw, don't worry about the giants. God promised He'd take care of them for us. We just have to go in and possess the land. That's all. Giants or not, the land is already ours because God said so."

But the two who were sold on the truth of God's Word were outvoted by the unbelieving majority who relied on their good common sense instead of on the promises of God.

What happened to the unbelievers? Did they get to enter the Promised Land anyway? No, God let every single one of them drop dead in the wilderness. Because they refused to believe what God told them, they perished. Joshua and Caleb were the only ones who survived to enter the Promised Land, many years later.

We need to understand something about unbelief so we won't goof our own chances of receiving all that God has promised and done for us.

Unbelief is not simply a lack of faith. Unbelief is a negative power generated by an act of will in the human head which says, "No, thank You, God. I want to do it my way. I'll believe the dead doctrines of men instead of trusting in Your living Word. Your way just doesn't sound reasonable to me; it just doesn't make sense. It sounds too supernatural, or something. Besides, my grandpa didn't believe like that, and he was a deacon in the church for forty years, so I won't believe that way either."

In physics, such negative power is known as bias. Bias voltage is very useful for control purposes in an electronic circuit. We can use it as a gate to stop the flow of positive power. We can use unbelief to stop the flow of God power, too.

Our human mechanism is like an electronic mechanism, a

bunch of electromagnetic wave patterns, and so is all the rest of creation as far as we know. At least, everything seems to behave in the way that electromagnetic wave patterns do.

When you, by an act of your will, inject the bias, the negative energy, of unbelief into the human mind, it closes down your mechanism of receptivity to God's Word. You become a blockhead—blocking yourself from God's best by your deliberate, willful negative bias.

In the biochemistry of the human heart, the bias, the negativity, of guilt, unforgiveness, and resentment can effectively paralyze the heart muscle so that it can no longer flex and pump blood. A heart on strike, not pumping the oxygen-bearing blood to every cell, doesn't do the rest of your body a whole lot of good, no matter how healthy it might have seemed to start with. Without oxygen, we lose in the game of life—fast.

According to chapter six of Paul's letter to the Ephesians, Christians are given a whole lot of armor—a girdle of truth, a breastplate of righteousness, footwear of the gospel of peace, a shield of faith, a helmet of salvation—and a weapon, the sword of the Spirit, to protect them from outside attacks by the enemy. But we can still be destroyed from the inside, from the negative bias we *let* settle in our hearts and minds to keep us from living it up in the eternal life Jesus died to give us.

The negativity of unforgiveness, guilt, and resentment can actually throw the heart mechanism out of synchronization. Guilt interferes with the voltages that control the heart action—the negative bias that God puts on it to hold it closed, the positive voltage that causes it to pulse in proper rhythm. A heart subjected to the strains of unforgiveness, guilt, fear, anxiety, and unrest suffers from scatter or random voltages and goes into all sorts of weird off-beat mutational pulsations, palpitations, and murmurings.

Captain Ralph Maxwell is a member of the Baltimore

County Fire Department and former director of its paramedical unit, a model copied by other units throughout the country. His outfit, trained in techniques for on-the-spot cardiac treatment for highway accident cases, utilizing radio-consultation with specialists in twenty-two area hospitals, has been responsible for saving many lives. Several years ago, Captain Maxwell wrote me:

> For the past several years, I have been responsible for training paramedical personnel to deliver Advanced Emergency Cardiac Care for the Baltimore Metropolitan Region. During this time, I have noted a definite connection between hardening of the spiritual heart and hardening of the arteries within the physical body.
>
> While there are several reasons for a person becoming a high-risk candidate for a heart attack, one in particular has interested me. Studies indicate that when a person lives under fear, worry, and stress, the body produces a higher than normal level of the hormone adrenalin within the bloodstream. When the adrenalin level within the body is excessive for prolonged periods of time, it pulls substances from the fatty tissues and produces a cholesterol buildup at an accelerated rate on the arterial walls, resulting in arteriosclerosis or hardening of the arteries.
>
> For the heart muscle to contract, it must be stimulated by an electrical impulse that originates near the top of the heart and spreads throughout the heart muscle, causing contraction. Hardening of the arteries causes irritability of the heart muscle which in turn can become a real threat to life itself.
>
> Several years ago, I placed a monitor on a heart patient to record his heart activity. He was instructed to keep a log of his activities and return for examination after eight

hours. Later, while evaluating his EKG, I found his heart
had produced a potentially life-threatening rhythm while
he was watching a world news report on national television.

The Bible says in Luke 21:26, "Men's hearts failing
them for fear and for looking after those things which are
coming on the earth." The Book of Hebrews (3:7–8) says,
"Today, if you will hear His voice, harden not your
hearts." How does one harden his spiritual heart toward
God? By permitting the things of this world and all its
concerns and interests to pass through his heart without
restriction. Then the heart loses its tenderness toward God
and becomes hardened, spiritually as well as physically.
But when the Word of God is received into the spiritual
heart by much meditation on His Word, the physical heart
is kept by the Spirit which produces peace, joy, and love
which are conducive to good health. When the Word of
God is shared with someone who refuses to receive it and
act upon it, that person actually hardens his heart toward
God, with detrimental results.

Even non-spiritual, unconverted cardiologists have doc-
umented proof that a person's chances of heart attack are
greatly increased when he or she is engaged in sexual ac-
tivity with someone else's husband or wife. Practicing
what is known to be against God's Word can produce not
only hardening of the arteries and heart attack, but many
other illnesses within the body.

"My heart panteth," the psalmist said. That's the best word
the Bible translators could think of to describe heart trouble
from the bad things we let settle in our gizzards. And modern
technology documents it—that when a man's heart is not right
toward God and his fellowman, trouble is building up inside.

But if we follow the plain instructions in the *Manufacturer's Handbook,* we'll be so forgiving of others, we'll confess our sins so regularly, that unforgiveness and guilt won't be in us. Our hearts will be free from the ravages of sin.

Heart trouble isn't the only ailment we can expect to have if we ignore the instructions God has given us for abundant life. Many painful cases of arthritis are known to have their origin in resentment. You turn a cold shoulder to someone, and your body can't stand the reduced temperature. Coldness causes calcium to settle in the joint. Arthritis sets in. Pretty soon, you can't raise your arm to wave good-bye or hello—even to someone you like.

Every instruction in the *Manufacturer's Handbook* is there that we might enjoy abundant life with Him forever—no aches, no pains, no frustration—all righteousness, peace and joy. That's what His Kingdom is made of.

Jesus summed up all the rules for us when He said, "Love God with all your heart and soul and mind—and love your neighbor as yourself."

"Oh," you say, "that sounds good, but I can never do it. Why, I can hardly even stand myself some days, let alone love anybody else."

Good! That's where the next step of the program comes in. God has made such excellent provision for your new creaturehood that He sends His own Holy Spirit to live in you, to give you power to live the kind of life you want to live now that you have been born again and have power to become a son of God.

What do you have to do to get this Holy Spirit?

All you have to do is ask.

12

You and the Holy Spirit

Time now to back up and review what we've said so far before we proceed with the rest of it.

In the beginning, God created. The evolutionist says that in the beginning, a little simple cell appeared out of nowhere and wriggled in a primordial swamp. There, after millions of years, it evolved into the human race of hairless apes. But the Second Law of Thermodynamics, a scientific law based on observable fact, says that there has never been an interchange of energy that did not come under the law of increasing disorder.

The Bible calls it the law of sin and death. You're stuck with degeneration, deterioration. From the day you're born, you begin to die.

Given enough time, says the evolutionist, we will evolve into something gloriously wonderful. Given enough time, says the Second Law of Physics, we will decay, degenerate, and fall apart. Heat never becomes hotter. The hot becomes cold; the light becomes dark; the living becomes dead. And in a few hundred years, the organized becomes disorganized. The simple never becomes the complex over a period of time, the theories of evolutionists to the contrary notwithstanding.

In an act of creation, God made man to have dominion over the rest of His creation. Our original parents blew that arrangement, but God reinstated it in Jesus. And now, having been born again, of the Spirit, by trusting Jesus, we know that living in the soul (mind and emotions) is death. All we had to live in, prior to our rebirth, were soul and body. We were two-dimensional, empty, dreary, drab corpses without Jesus. We had length and width, but no depth at all. Before Jesus, we were shallow people. There is no depth or capacity for God in a two-dimensional corpse.

But once we have received Jesus, we are alive in God because we have been born again in Jesus Christ. And Jesus in us is the Light of the world.

The Bible says we have this treasure—this priceless treasure, Jesus—in earthen vessels (2 Corinthians 4:7). We are the vessels, He is the treasure. Once upon a time I had sort of looked at it this way—that if you could cut me open and look within, you'd find Jesus down inside there in a little velvet-lined compartment. But one day recently, I saw that Jesus actually suffuses every atom of our beings. He's not down inside in just one little pocket. If you could slice open every single atom of your body, you'd find Jesus in the nucleus of every one. Without Him there, you'd find total torment. You would see more empty space than anything else, because according to the classical diagram, an atom consists of orbiting shells of electrons spaced far apart from each other. Scientists have said that the total effect is about like standing out in the open on a starry night and looking into the heavens. The distance between you and the farthest star represents the empty space between the nucleus of an atom and the outer electron shell. Vast emptiness surrounds the nucleus—until Jesus comes in to fill all things according to His promise in Ephesians 1:23. Before that happens, before your regeneration, every atom of your being is trying to explode, to blow up. One of the greatest mysteries among secular scientists, scientists without knowledge of God, is "Why doesn't the atom explode the instant it's formed because of this tremendous explosive energy built in?"

The Bible is the only textbook I own that explains that Jesus is the binding power that holds the atom together.

You're an explosive bomb, a mixture of turmoil and misery, until Jesus moves in. That's why human beings are so often repulsive to one another. Coulomb's Law of Mutual Repulsion is built into every atom, and into every one of us.

After we're born again, the repelling principle is reversed, and Jesus pulls us together. Every man-made fellowship has a tendency to fall apart. We try to glue them together with circuses and bake sales and clambakes and hoe-downs and fix-ups and all kinds of make-work things. But when we become born again and Spirit-filled, you can't keep us apart. Jesus holds us together in proper order and union. We are complete in him (Colossians 210). Our orbits are filled out, satisfied, by Jesus and only by Him.

Being born again is not just a subjective experience, it's a demonstrable scientific fact. There is actually a scientific instrument that can detect whether or not you are born again, whether or not you have Jesus, the Light of the world, in you. A lecturer I once heard, Dr. Donald Liebman, has developed what I call a glory meter.

Dr. Liebman is a "completed Jew," one who has met Jesus as his Messiah—his Saviour and Baptizer in the Holy Spirit. The laboratory instrument he developed is used in brain research to measure the energy within the human mechanism. It can calibrate the light, the energy level, within your structure

prior to your rebirth, after your rebirth, and after you have
been baptized with the Holy Spirit. There are remarkable dif-
ferences!

When you're born into this world, the light that lighteth
every man coming into this world (John 1:9) measures between
eight and ten on Dr. Liebman's scale, way down on the bottom
end. It's just enough to get you moving, to start you off, a
booster shot that lasts long enough to get you born again. But if
you're stupid enough or stubborn enough to avoid or evade
that second birth, you'll soon find out that the booster shot
wasn't designed to get you very far down the road of life.
You'll begin to peter out in your seventh year, and by the time
you're forty, you'll be living on chemical additives to keep the
corpse quivering. Pagans live their lives in that land of darkness, close by the gates of death, just barely alive, and Dr.
Liebman's instrument can detect it.

When you say yes to Jesus, and He moves in, not as an in-
tellectual idea in your head, but as a living reality in your
heart, down where you live, the meter reading goes up between
fifty and sixty, above the middle of the dial. You're born again,
a new creature, a baby Christian, really alive. According to
John 1:12, when you received Him, He gave you the power—
the energy—to become a son of God.

Jesus didn't present the born-again experience as an option.
He said it was an absolute necessity. 'Ye *must* be born again"
(John 3:7, *italics mine*). The born-again experience is not just a
good thing. It's not to make you good. It's to make you alive!
You're just plain dead without it.

But that's not all. There's another step—the baptism in the
Holy Spirit. Before we have that, we are half-scale Christians,
half-baked, half-power, like an automobile with half the cylin-
ders taken out of the engine. Oh, you'll clunk along, but you
won't have a smooth ride, and you won't really get anywhere

or be able to help anyone else much along the way. You'll certainly not win the race.

In John 1:29, 33 we read, "Behold the Lamb of God, which taketh away the sin of the world. . . . the same is he which baptizeth with the Holy Ghost." Luke 3:16 says, ". . . He shall baptize you with the Holy Ghost and with fire." Matthew and Mark say about the same thing. Jesus saves us, and Jesus baptizes us, two distinct and separate functions which sometimes occur simultaneously, depending on how far you sold out to Jesus in the beginning.

As our living Saviour, Jesus Christ comes into us through a personal encounter. He energizes our body, brings us to life, and then He says, "I'd like to baptize you in My Holy Spirit. I'd like to give you power, and energize you to be My witness."

The reading on Dr. Liebman's meter zooms up over a hundred, to the top of the scale when it's hooked up to a born-again, Spirit-baptized Christian. Dr. Liebman's going to have to make the scale longer, because it's too short to measure the total energy in that kind of lit-up Christian. The word *Christian* really means "little anointed one." Isn't it something that an objective scientific instrument can recognize the anointing!

For clarification: All Christians are baptized *by* the Holy Spirit *into* the body of Christ when they're born again (1 Corinthians 12:13). That's the baptism *of* the Holy Spirit. The baptism by Jesus *in* (or *with*) the Holy Spirit takes place when we go to Jesus for the second transaction (Luke 3:16). When that happens, the Holy Ghost comes upon us (Acts 1:8), we receive power—and we become His witnesses.

When we receive the Holy Spirit in His fullness, we don't have to *choose* to be witnesses; it's an automatic thing. Jesus said, "Ye *shall* be witnesses unto me." No ifs or buts about it. A witness is somebody who sees something, and the Holy Spirit opens our eyes to who God is and what He's doing. Whether your natural vision is 20/20 or you need a seeing-eye dog, when you are baptized in the Holy Spirit, you'll be like Peter and John when they said, "We cannot but speak of the things which we have seen and heard" (Acts 4:20), because the Holy Spirit opens your eyes and reveals God to you (Ephesians 1:17–19).

You think maybe the Holy Spirit is not for you? When Peter stood up to preach on the day of Pentecost, he quoted the prophet Joel who quoted God as saying, "I will pour out of my Spirit upon *all* flesh . . . ," (Acts 2:17, *italics mine*). That "all flesh" probably includes you, unless you're made of plastic or some other synthetic. And when his congregation asked him what they could do to get right with God, Peter told them to repent, to be baptized, and they would ". . . receive the gift of the Holy Ghost. For the promise is unto you, and to your children, and to all that are afar off, even as many as the Lord our God shall call" (Acts 2:38, 39). Sounds like that could include you, too, doesn't it?

Sometimes people try to weasel out of qualifying for a top score on Liebman's glory meter by saying, "I'm too much for God to handle."

Forget it. All have sinned and come short of the glory of God. You've no right to think you're that much worse than the rest of us. And really, when you consider it, a corpse is not too hard to handle anyhow. It doesn't have much resistance left in it. All you have to do is give up and abandon all your do-it-yourself schemes. Ask Jesus to take over, and stop trying to understand what's going to happen. Then, watch it happen. New creaturehood—not while you wait—but ZAP, just like that, in the twinkling of an eye, at the speed of light. Not because you're worthy—but because God loves you!

In one of John's letters, he sums it up for us:

See what [an incredible] quality of love the Father has given ... us, that we should [be ...] ... the children of God! and so we are! ... Beloved, we are ... now God's children; it is not yet disclosed ... what we shall be [hereafter], but we know that when He comes, ... we shall ... be like Him, for we shall see Him just as He [really] is.

1 John 3:1, 2 AMP

That's not evolution; that's being changed from glory to glory as we look at Him, the One who created us in His image.

What a future is in store for us who believe in Him, who are called to be King's kids in the here and now.

In the fullness of the Spirit of God, all frustration is gone. Everything is in equilibrium and at rest. All forces are balanced. This is the power of the Holy Spirit. As you approach the speed of light, things slow down. At the speed of light, things stand still, and beyond the speed of light, some scientists speculate that things might run backward. We don't know for sure, because we haven't gone that fast yet.

God is light. In Him, there is no change. The laws of physics and the laws of science and the Bible fit together perfectly because our God is the overall designer. You don't have to show the ravages of time if you're resting in the rest that remains for the people of God.

Time is reversible up and down the scale at the point of light where God is. He can run backward or forward, because at the speed of light, there is the timelessness of eternity. God spoke about it long ago when He said, "Before they call, I will answer. And while you're yet speaking will I hear, if you're walking in the light" (Isaiah 65:24, *author's paraphrase*). We're discovering things every day in the world of science that God put in His book thousands of years ago. (*See* Appendix II for some of them.)

There are many things in the Bible that we can't understand as yet, but they're true just the same. All that proves is that God knows more than we do. But He's revealing many things to us as we go along. The next revelation is always just around the corner, as soon as we're sufficiently mature to handle it.

The first verse of chapter nine of the Book of Revelation has been mysterious to us until very recently: "And the fifth angel sounded, and I saw a star fall from heaven unto the earth, and to him was given the key to the bottomless pit." Not long ago, astronomers discovered something like a bottomless pit, 'way up in the north sky.

Radio waves aimed in that direction are absorbed. Light beams are absorbed. Everything that goes into that pit is swallowed up; it disappears completely—without a trace, into a big black hole. To me, it sounds like the bottomless pit referred to in Revelation.

Scientists theorize that there might have been a tremendous heavenly body—at least three times the size of our sun—that suddenly collapsed, leaving a tremendous force of gravity without mass. Such a gravitational force would suck into itself every thing it could, just like a powerful vacuum cleaner. The garbage disposal system of the universe, you could call it. Someday Satan is going to be tossed into a bottomless pit, a black hole (Revelation 20:1-3).

It sounds scary, and these days, pagans *are* running scared. But King's kids are not going to have to deal with those things. They're involved with light, because God is light, and in Him is no darkness at all. Darkness is actually the lack of anything, the absence of energy, the absence of light. Light is energy. Light is real. It behaves like matter. And when we are centered in Jesus, when we are walking in the Spirit, when we are in contact with God, we are within a circle of light, protected from the enemy. Satan can't put a finger on King's kids; he can't talk them into eating any bad apples as long as they make choices that enable them to stay in the light.

At the speed of light, life processes stand still. God says, "I am the eternal one. I change not. I am that I am."

We discovered something interesting about timelessness when we sent the astronauts into outer space. When the Apollo astronauts came back from their thirteenth mission, they reportedly calculated the amount of money that they should refund to the government because they spent less time on their round trip than we spent on the earth waiting for them.

The faster you go, the less time it takes to make a trip. If we can send a space vehicle out into space at a hundred and eighty thousand miles per second, we can visit a galaxy 50 trillion miles away and come back in a round trip of seventy years. While the astronauts are traveling the total elapsed time of seventy years, the earth will age 3 million years. At the speed of light, there is no aging at all.

We're bringing in intelligent radio signals from outer space continually by way of radio telescopes, and we are recording them.[1] We can't translate them as yet, but one of these days, we hope to acquire at least a little bit of knowledge compared to the folks who are sending the signals. When we are able to decode them, we may find the people from outer space on some other planet saying, "Earth people, why don't you get with it? Why do you stay so stupid? Why don't you ask Jesus to become your wisdom, your righteousness, your sanctification, and redemption? [*See* 1 Corinthians 1:30]. You have cooked up a system of theology and religion which has a form of godliness but denies the power thereof. Why don't you really get with it? Why don't you turn on to Jesus?"

Lots of opinions are being expressed these days by lots of

thinkers about the possibility of another life after this life. Most of the opinions I have heard have been based on religious beliefs, philosophical ideas, or just plain ignorance. And because conflicting reports have come from persons who reportedly came back from the dead, it's hard for some people to know where to go for the right information.

Bible believers already know what God says about such things, that most folks are going to die but after that there will be a resurrection and we will all live forever somewhere. If you are not too impressed with the Bible, look at what the laws of science have to say about it.

"Hold it a cotton pickin' minute, Hill!" I hear someone sputtering. "Are you telling me that down-to-earth scientific laws have something to say about how I spend eternity?"

That's exactly what I am telling you, and here's how it works. The first law of science, the Law of Energy Conservation, otherwise known as the First Law of Thermodynamics flatly states that it is impossible to either create or destroy energy. We started out in the beginning with a fixed amount of the stuff and we will end up with exactly the same amount at the windup of the earth system. All of it will still be around somewhere, in usable or "used" form (entropy, remember?).

The Second Law of Thermodynamics says that all energy, in whatever form we find it, can be transformed into other states by proper manipulation. The Second Law also says that during the transformation of energy, some of it becomes unavailable and goes into the bank account of unavailability, low-grade energy, too lukewarm to do anyone any good.

Now, what are you made of?

"Cells and other stuff," some brave soul ventures. That's true, but there's more to it than that—the electromagnetic wave patterns or energy that makes your cells function. In other words, the "live" you is an invisible energy system that

cannot be created or destroyed. According to the laws of thermodynamics, the energy part of you is going to be hanging
around forever somewhere in one form or another, like it or
not. One day your earthenware body will rot away, but the real
you, released from your old body at the time of your "death"
will merely take off into another dimension.

"That sounds spooky, Hill. I'm not sure I'm ready for all
that." But ready or not, that's what will happen. As soon as the
real you leaves the flesh-and-bones cage, the real you will show
up in another dimension. The laws of thermodynamics guarantee it. But the matter of where you'll spend the rest of forever is
left entirely up to you. You may choose to spend your eternity
in the good place, heaven, where there is no sickness or crying
and where everybody is so rich the streets are paved with gold.
Or you may choose to spend it in hell where there's no air con-
ditioning or anything else to recommend it.

Limited to those two options, only somebody who didn't
understand he had a choice would choose the bad place. Now
that you know the truth about these things, it's time for all in-
habitants of planet earth to get with it.

Indeed, it *is* time for us all to get with it—to become Jesus-
centered persons, ready for His return. If you read carefully the
biblical prophecies about the things that must happen before
the second coming of Jesus, you can know that most of them
have already been fulfilled. The fact that He is coming again is
as reliable as the fact that He came in the first place. It is time
for each man to choose between the one who will be thrown
into the blackness of the bottomless pit and the One who will
rule forever and ever in the kingdom of light.

You can settle all doubts about *your* future—right now.
Your place in the "good place" with Jesus forever will be reserved for you as you pray this prayer:

Lord Jesus Christ, please come into my heart right now and save me. Wash away all that filthiness, guilt, and fear down inside where I live. Purify me with Your shed blood and wash me whiter than snow. Make me a completely new person and fill that awful, empty, God-shaped hole with Yourself. Come and live inside me. Live Your life through me, beginning now and continuing forever.

Thank You for Your beautiful peace and assurance that my record is gone, that I'm right with God, and that from now on, I can look to You, knowing that You are in charge of my life and affairs. Change me to suit Yourself. Help Yourself to me completely. And if I'm not sincere in all this—please just go ahead and do it *anyhow.* Thank You, Jesus. Amen.

King's kid, you have just claimed your inheritance as a son of God! Sign your name and date on the dotted line below, recording for history that today you became a King's kid. Get your friends to turn in their raunchy lives for brand-new ones, too, and sign their names along with yours. Then write me a note to let me in on the good news of the brand-new additions to the Kingdom of the King. Address Harold Hill, King's Kids' Korner, P.O. Box 8655, Baltimore, MD 21240.

Name . . . .   Date . . . .
Name . . . .   Date . . . .
Name . . . .   Date . . . .
Name . . . .   Date . . . .

Learn more about *How to Live Like a King's Kid* by reading the book with that title available from the above address.

Appendix I
Things Apes Never Do
or
How Human Behavior Differs From That of Other Creatures

The Bible (Genesis 1:26, 27) says that God made man in His own image and that He gave him dominion over all the other creatures. If that is true, we ought to be able to observe it. In fact, the behavioral scientist Adler has already observed it for us and nicely catalogued his findings. They were published in the following convenient list in the *Bible-Science Newsletter* (November, 1975):

1. Only man employs a propositional language, only man uses verbal symbols, only man makes sentences; i.e., only man is a discursive animal.
2. Only man makes tools, builds fires, erects shelters, fabricates clothing, i.e., only man is a technological animal.
3. Only man enacts laws or sets up his own rules of behavior and thereby constitutes his social life, organizing his association with his fellows in a variety of different ways, i.e., only man is a political, not just a gregarious animal.
4. Only man has developed, in the course of generations, a cumulative cultural tradition, the transmission of which constitutes human history, i.e., only man is a historical animal.
5. Only man engages in magical ritualistic practices, i.e., only man is a religious animal.
6. Only man has a moral conscience, a sense of right and wrong, and of values, i.e., only man is an ethical animal.
7. Only man decorates or adorns himself or his artifacts, and makes pictures or statues for the nonutilitarian purpose of enjoyment, i.e., only man is an esthetic animal.

Man has unique traits that distinguish him from other animals and this evidence agrees with God's revealed Word.

Appendix II
A Few Scientific Facts the Bible Knew Before the Eggheads Caught On

Evolution is impossible, because every seed reproduces its own genus:

> And the earth brought forth grass, and herb yielding *seed after his kind,* and the tree yielding fruit, whose seed was in itself, *after his kind.* . . . And God created great whales, and every living creature that moveth, which the waters brought forth abundantly, *after their kind,* and every winged fowl *after his kind.* . . . And God said, Let the earth bring forth the living creature *after his kind,* cattle, and creeping thing, and the beast of the earth *after his kind.* . . .
> Genesis 1:12, 21, 24, *italics mine*

There is great wealth in the sea:

195

. . . The abundant wealth of the [Dead] Sea shall be turned to you. . . .

Isaiah 60:5 AMP

[A footnote in the Amplified Bible explains:

Prior to well in the twentieth century, scholars could only speculate as to what Isaiah could have meant here by "the abundant wealth of the Sea" that was one day to be turned over to Jerusalem. . . . The Dead . . . Sea for ages had been considered only a place of death and desolation. . . . Then suddenly it was discovered that the waters of the Dead Sea contained important chemicals. In 1935 A.D., G. T. B. Davis wrote in his *Rebuilding Palestine,* "One is almost staggered by the computed wealth of the chemical salts in the Dead Sea. It is estimated that the potential value of the potash, bromine, and other chemical salts of the waters is . . . four times the wealth of the United States!" Isaiah himself did not know this, but the God who made the Dead Sea for a part in His end-time program knew all about it, and caused this record to say so.]

Light involves motion:

Where is the *way* where light dwells? . . .

Job 38:19 AMP, *italics mine*

[Here again, the Amplified Bible explains:

How, except by divine inspiration, could Job have known that light does not dwell in a *place,* but a *way?* For light, as modern man has discovered, involves motion, wave motion, and traveling 186,000 miles a second, it can only dwell in a *way.*]

There are currents in the ocean:

The birds of the air, and the fish of the sea, and whatever passes along the *paths of the seas.*

Psalms 8:8 AMP, *italics mine*

There is a hydrographic circulatory system on this planet:

... Who calls for waters of the sea, and pours them out upon the face of the earth. ...

Amos 5:8 AMP

All streams flow into the sea,
yet the sea is never full.

To the place the streams come from,
there they return again.

Ecclesiastes 1:7 NIV

Energy becomes unusable (the Law of Increasing Entropy):

In the beginning you laid the foundations of the earth,
   and the heavens are the work of your hands.
They will perish, but you remain;
   they will all wear out like a garment. ...

Psalms 102:25, 26 NIV

The earth is poised in space:

He it is Who spreads out the northern skies over emptiness and hangs the earth upon or over nothing.

Job 26:7 AMP

The world is round:

It is God Who sits above the circle (the horizon) of the earth. . . .

Isaiah 40:22 AMP

Blood circulates all through the human body:

The life of the flesh is in the blood. . . .

Leviticus 17:11

[In the seventeenth century, William Harvey discovered that blood circulates throughout the entire human body.]

Everything is made of invisible energy:

By faith we understand that the universe was formed at God's command, so that what is seen was not made out of what was visible.

Hebrews 11:3 NIV

There is music coming from the stars, now detectable by scientific instruments as a shrill, creaking sound:

When the morning stars sang together. . . .

Job 38:7 AMP

There is an infinite number of stars:

As the host of heaven cannot be numbered. . . .

Jeremiah 33:22

[Human wisdom had said, "There are exactly 1,026 stars" (Hipparchus 150 B.C.); "The total of the stars is 1,056" (Ptolemy, at the time of Christ); "They can't be numbered" (Galileo A.D. 1610, looking through a telescope).]

The stars are not pure:

. . . yea, the stars are not pure in his sight.

Job 25:5

[The ancient notion that the stars are pure was first refuted by Galileo when he observed sunspots through the telescope.]

High explosives can be safely shipped in shaved ice:

Hast thou entered into the treasures of the snow? or hast thou seen the treasures of the hail, Which I have reserved against the time of trouble, against the day of battle and war?

Job 38:22, 23

[During World War I, we were having trouble controlling high explosives. They were being detonated by the ship's motion. A Jewish scientist who sought God for the answer to the problem was given the directive, "Pack them in shaved ice." It solved the problem.]

The First Law of Thermodynamics is that nothing is being created or destroyed:

Thus the heavens and the earth were finished, and all the host of them.

Genesis 2:1

By the same word the present heavens and earth are reserved for fire, being kept for the day of judgment. . . .

2 Peter 3:7 NIV

Appendix III
Egghead Opinions of Yesteryear,
or
So Much for Human Wisdom

The following quotations are taken from the "Never Say Never" sections of the January/February, 1984, issue of *Science* magazine, pages 37, 39, 42.

In 1945 Vannevar Bush, the chief of the federal government's Office of Scientific Research and Development, dealt with the notion of using rockets to deliver bombs. "Such a thing is impossible," he said, "and will be impossible for many years. The people who have been writing about these things have been talking about a 3,000 mile high angle rocket shot from one continent to another carrying an atomic bomb, and so directed as to be a precise weapon which would land exactly on a . . . city. I say, technically, I don't think anybody in the world knows how to do such a thing, and I feel confident it will not be done for a very long period of time to come." Twelve years later the Soviet Union test fired the first ICBM.

"The abolishment of pain in surgery is a chimera. It is absurd to go on seeking it today. *Knife* and *pain* are two words in surgery that must forever be associated in the consciousness of the patient. To this compulsory combination we shall have to adjust ourselves."—Dr. Alfred Velpeau, 1839, seven years before anesthesia was introduced.

"While theoretically and technically television may be feasible, commercially and financially I consider it an impossibility, a development of which we need waste little time dreaming."—Lee DeForest, U.S. inventor and "Father of the Radio," 1926.

"At present few scientists foresee any serious or practical use for atomic energy. They regard the atom-splitting experiments as useful steps in the attempt to describe the atom more accurately, not as the key to the unlocking of any new power."—*Fortune,* 1938.

"What can be more palpably absurd than the prospect held out of locomotives traveling twice as fast as stagecoaches?"—*The Quarterly Review,* 1825.

"The ordinary 'horseless carriage' is at present a luxury for the wealthy; and although its price will probably fall in the future, it will never, of course, come into as common use as the bicycle."—*The Literary Digest,* October 14, 1889.

"The energy necessary to propel the ship would be many times greater than that required to drive a train of cars at the same speed; hence as a means of rapid transit, aerial navigation could not begin to compete with the railroad."—William Baxter, Jr., *Popular Science,* 1897.

"I must confess that my imagination . . . refuses to see any sort of submarine doing anything but suffocating its crew and floundering at sea."—H. G. Wells, British novelist, in *Anticipations,* 1901.

Appendix IV
Whatever Happened to the Hittites?

Who were the Hittites? What do they have to do with us King's kids who praise the Lord and brag on Jesus as a part of our daily routine?

Well, for many centuries Dr. Tinkling Cymbal and Professor Sounding Brass declared that the Bible was an interesting historical document that a young man must study if he wanted to be a minister with a degree from his particular ceme—er, ah, sorry, I mean—seminary.

But *believe* the Bible? Well, that's a charming idea, very sentimental but hardly scholarly. You see, the Bible is just a book of legendary stories, which do contain some historical truths, but so-o-o many inaccuracies. Well, it's just not to be trusted. Too many loose details.

Take the Hittites for example.

"We know for certain that such a people *never* existed," pronounced Dr. Bigbrain ponderously. "Archaeologists have found *no* evidence of them, no pottery, no burial grounds, no edifices, nothing. The Hittites were just a figment of God's imagination."

Of course the Bible does refer to the Hittites as occupying the Land of Canaan during Abraham's time (*see* Genesis 15:20). After his wife Sarah died, he needed a burial plot, so he purchased a piece of land from a man named Ephron the Hittite (*see* Genesis 23:3–20). "Probably it is just a scribe's error in copying the Scriptures since we know that the Hittites are an Abrahamic aberration," the Eggheads would explain.

We next run into the "nonexisting" Hittites when Esau married two Hittite girls (*see* Genesis 26:34) and then when the Lord gave Joshua and the children of Israel their marching orders to cross over the Jordan River into the Promised Land.

"Get up and go, Joshua!" the Lord commanded. "What you can see is what you get! From the wilderness (Sinai desert in the south) to Lebanon (in the north), from the great river Euphrates (in the east) to the great (Mediterranean) Sea (in the west)—*all the land of the Hittites* [*italics mine*], it's all yours! Go and take it!" (*See* Joshua 1:4.) The Lord was giving Joshua and the children of Israel the entire country of the Hittites! What a shame. Somebody should have told the Lord God Almighty that He was bestowing upon His beloved inheritance merely a miraculous mirage.

And anyway it seemed that the Lord had an enormous grudge against these poor, imaginary people for no reason at all. He was always ordering the Israelites to destroy them: "Wipe them off the face of the earth! Put them all to the sword! All the men, women, children, animals, all of them! Make no peace agreements with them! Show no mercy!" (*See* Joshua 6:17, 21; 8:2, 8, 26; 10:28, 30, 32, 33, 37, 39, 40; 11:11, 12, 14, 21, and so on.)

Wow! It's a good thing that the Hittites were an hallucination, or they would have fallen into the hands of a cruel, angry God.

There is one good thing, however, about the Hittites being a so-called biblical boo-boo: it lets David off the hook with his shenanigans with Bathsheba. Bathsheba was taking a bath, you remember, when David leered at her from his palace balcony. The way the Bible tells it, Bathsheba was a no-no because she was married to Uriah the Hittite. Well, lucky for David, the Hittites are a denominational delusion, a fact which makes a marriage to Bathsheba fair game and further crumbles the credibility of large portions of the Word of God.

The last time we hear of the "make-believe" Hittites in the Bible we see that God is on their case again. He even uses their name as a curse when He wants to put down idol-worshiping Jerusalem: "Your father was an Amorite and your mother was a Hittite!" As far as God was concerned, that was the worst thing He could have called them!

And then silence. For centuries nothing was said about the Hittites, and the memory of them faded into the past. Scholars discounted their very existence, saying that even if some Hittite tribes did exist, they were a small, insignificant part of the Canaanites. As the *Encyclopaedia Britannica* puts it, "Prior to the advent of modern historical scholarship the notion and very name of the Hittites ... the total knowledge of the 'Hittites' ... was derived from the Old Testament. ..."

At the same time, travelers and residents in the north central part of Turkey, near a city with the tongue-twisting name of Boghazkoy, marveled at the magnificent carvings on the rocks of the mountains.

Similar to the figures on Mount Rushmore, these remarkable monuments show the meeting of two kings, each followed by a train of soldiers and lackeys. One king is wearing a tight-fitting dress with a high pointed cap, like a witch's hat, and is sporting a long beard. The other king is dressed in loose-flowing robes, like a muumuu, with a square turreted hat, and is without a beard.

"Who put those there?" the vacationers asked, and the answer varied according to the college major of the Egghead talking.

"They were the Lydians and Medes signing a peace treaty!" said one sage.

"No, I disagree. They are the Babylonians and the Assyrians, having a confrontation!" pronounced another pundit.

"Maybe they are the Hittites of the Bible?" ventured a knowledgeable King's kid. (Yes, God has had a few King's kids in strategic positions throughout the ages. Remember Daniel and Esther?)

"Hittites! Only in the Bible! Ha, ha, ha!" scoffed the profs. "Everybody knows the Bible isn't accurate. Look at that story about Jonah in the belly of a whale. You can't be serious?"

So for centuries, whenever an unbeliever wanted to take potshots at the accuracy of the Bible, he would bring up the "nebulous" nation of the Hittites.

But in 1799, near the city of Rosetta in Egypt, one of Napoleon's soldiers, digging around in the dirt, found a black stone on which were a lot of bird's feet impressions. This piece of basalt, now called the Rosetta Stone, unlocked the mystery of hieroglyphics. Not bird's feet at all, an unimportant message, written in three different languages, enabled scholars to translate back and forth from Greek to hieroglyphics to demotic, the common language of the Egyptians.

It was one of the greatest discoveries since the world began, and now for the first time Egyptian hieroglyphics could be translated. It took a while to make out the carvings on the temples and monuments all over the land of Egypt, but once they were understood, lo and behold, there were the Hittites! One of the mightiest empires of the world, the Hittite people occupied the lands we now call Turkey, Syria, and Iraq, spreading even as far south as Lebanon and parts of Israel, reigning as world power from 1600 B.C. to 1200 B.C.

Now we are beginning to get a picture in our minds about who lives where during this crucial period in Bible history. Imagine, if you will, the Middle East with Egypt under Pharaoh Ramses II to the far south. Then around the Mediterranean Sea to the north lay the mighty Hittite empire. Directly between them lay the Promised Land. The very land that God promised to give to Abraham was strategically placed between these two giants. Around 1300 B.C. Pharaoh Ramses II led an army north to win back Syria from the Hittites. At a spot in northern Lebanon, called Kadesh, he was ambushed by the Hittites. He rallied his men with fierce courage and cut his way out. Though the battle was far from a victory, Ramses proudly recorded it on the walls of various temples in Egypt.

Shortly after, Ramses and the Hittite king drew up a treaty. Two copies of the treaty have been found in Egypt, and another among the ancient public records of the Hittite capital in Turkey, Boghazkoy. The document called thousands of gods to witness and divided Syria between the Egyptians and the Hittites, arranging for the two countries to defend each other in case of attack. Peace now reigned from the north to the south between these two weakened world powers.

The mystery of the mountain-carved figures near Boghazkoy also was solved. Clean-shaven Ramses and the bearded Hittite king, plus their armies and servants, had been there all the time. While various wiseacres had been claiming the nonexistence of the Hittites, the ancient hills told a different story.

The stage was set for the Exodus.

No one could have known at the time that this famous clash

between the Egyptians and the Hittites was God's plan to remove all obstacles by so weakening these nations that His King's kids, who were slaving away making bricks without straw down in Egypt, could escape. It would not be too long before both of these great nations would decline as world powers, but in the interval the land of Canaan (which would soon be Israel) was relatively peaceful and subdued.

"So get up and *go,* Joshua!" commanded the Lord. "Cross over the Jordan into Canaan! No man shall be able to defeat you! You are well able to take it because I have gone before you and prepared the way!"

God's ways are so far above our ways that we can only marvel at the lengthy preparations that He designed and executed over a period of years—an intricate plan that would result in the removal of almost 2 million people from one country and their placement in another. Read about it in the Book of Exodus.

Our God is a loving God who makes good on His promises. Israel has yet to achieve ownership of *all the land of the Hittites,* which God pledged to Joshua, but the end of the story has not been written.

"But what about those terrible commands that God gave to His generals in the Old Testament?" someone may ask. "How can you say He is a loving God when He ordered the complete destruction of entire nations, even their children and animals? That doesn't seem very loving to me."

This morning the mailman brought the answer to your question, the latest issue of the *Biblical Archaeology Review,* showing color photographs of the charred bones and remains of little children—newborns, infants, and toddlers—contained in urns in a cemetery which has recently been unearthed at Carthage, and another one near Jerusalem. These are just two examples of cemeteries all over the ancient world containing the remains of little victims of child sacrifice. The article says:

> Out of reverence for Ba'al ... whenever they [parents] seek to obtain some great favor, they vow one of their children, burning it as a sacrifice to the deity. There stands in their midst a bronze statue of the god, its hands extended over a bronze brazier, the flames of which engulf the child. When the flames fall upon the body, the limbs contract and the open mouth seems almost to be laughing, until the contracted body slips quietly into the brazier. Thus it is that the "grin" is known as "sardonic laughter" since they die "laughing." ... Their own parents offered them to him (the god) ... and fondled them that they might not be sacrificed in tears.[1]

Jeremiah nailed it down by prophesying:

> "The people of Judah have done evil in my eyes, declares the Lord. ... They have built the high places of Topheth in the Valley of Ben Hinnom to burn their sons and daughters in the fire—something I did not command nor did it enter my mind. So beware, the days are coming, declares the Lord, when people will no longer call it Topheth or the Valley of Ben Hinnom, but the Valley of Slaughter, for they will bury the dead in Topheth. ...
>   Jeremiah 7:30–32 NIV (*see also* Jeremiah 32:30–35)

Topheth was the place near Jerusalem where Ba'al worship took place and the bodies of the little children were buried.
    Another horrible ritual the pagans practiced was what they called "foundation sacrifices." When a house was to be built, a child would be sacrificed and its body built into the wall, to

bring good luck to the rest of the family. Do you know where the word *luck* comes from? From Lucifer. Satan, who was having a ball, killing all those little children! He knew that one of those little children would be the very one God would use to clobber him. He didn't know *which one,* so he killed as many as he could.

In excavations at Megiddo, the ruins of a temple of Ashtoreth, goddess wife of Ba'al, were found. Nearby was a cemetery full of the remains of infants who had been burned in the temple. Prophets of Ba'al and Ashtoreth were official murderers of little children, a fact which may bring better understanding of Elijah's execution of the false prophets.

Canaanites worshiped by murdering their children and having official mass sex orgies—all in the name of religion. Do we wonder any longer why God commanded Israel to exterminate them? Did a "civilization" of such brutality have any right to exist? Archaeologists, digging in the ruins of the Canaanite cities, are amazed that God did not destroy them sooner than He did.

The reason God commanded the destruction of the Canaanites begins to be understood. His object, besides being a judgment on the Canaanites, was to keep Israel from the same idolatrous sins. His one grand specific purpose was to pave the way for the coming of His Son, Jesus, by establishing in the world the *idea* that there is only one true living God. If Israel fell into the same sins as her neighbors (and she did), then there was no longer any reason for her to exist as a nation.

Joshua gave Israel a good start by cleaning up much of the idolatrous worship in the land. If only Israel had continued with it, what a different story there would be to tell!

But, wait a minute. God has a habit of making a message out of a mess. While He temporarily turned His back on the Israelites, scattering them among the nations for centuries, the scarlet thread, the royal blood line leading to the birth of Jesus, was miraculously preserved. Read the Book of Esther for a spine-chilling account of how one woman saved the Jewish race from total extinction.

But God did get His Man into the world, at a time and in a place where Satan least expected it. Preceded by many false messiahs to further confuse Satan, Jesus of Nazareth, the future King of kings, was born in a barn in Bethlehem. And God had prepared the way again: Alexander the Great had given the civilized world one common language, Greek; the Romans laid down paved roads all over the Bible regions; and the Pax Romana, peace enforced by Rome, prevailed on the earth—just the right conditions for spreading the Good News.

"Good news!" God says, "I have good news for you! Listen to Me and you will have a good life. Follow My instructions and they will lead you to *real living*.

"When you learn what I have planned for you, how much I want your company, the happy, healthy, and prosperous lifestyle I intend for you, you'll want to join up with me now!" God says.

"Sickness, suffering, fear, guilt, despair, defeat, poverty—these are not my desire for you! Satan will try to kill you with these things, but I have outflanked him. I have a secret weapon, My Son, Jesus. I have put Him on the earth in order to destroy the works of the devil and to restore you to Myself. I have missed you! I love you! I love you so much that I have ordered My Son to take all the punishment due you for your wrongdoings. He will die in your place. And you will go *free!*

"Only believe this, and you enter into the *good life!* Then go tell others! But hurry! There isn't much time left! I'm about to bring the Church Age to an end. Jesus is here in heaven with Me now, but I'm getting ready to send Him back to gather up His brothers and sisters on the earth. Soon you'll hear a loud blast of a trumpet, and a mighty shout! Jesus will be calling His church! The end of all things is near. Are you waiting for Him? I'm waiting for you!" says the Lord.

Don't put it off any longer, dear reader. Lay down this book, and go alone to your room. Kneel down beside your bed. Tell Jesus that you are sorry for the life you've led without Him and ask Him to come in and make His home with you. Ask Him to lead you and guide you for the rest of your life. Give Him all your troubles, all your cares, all your problems. He will take them, and in exchange He will give you the Good Life. You will have a new start. You can begin again! All you have to do is to praise Him and thank Him for doing it.

Congratulations! You're a King's kid now. Keep on praising the Lord for the rest of your life.

Appendix V
Bibliography on Creationism

The following reading list is taken from *Scientific Creationism,* prepared by the technical staff and consultants of the Institute for Creation Research; edited by Henry M. Morris (San Diego: Creation-Life Publishers, 1974).

The books and periodicals listed below are recommended for all school libraries in order to provide students and teachers access to a fair sample of the available literature on scientific creationism.

I. *Books by creationist scientists emphasizing the scientific aspects of creationism.*

Barnes, Thomas G., *Origin and Destiny of the Earth's Magnetic Field* (San Diego: Institute for Creation Research, 1973), 64 pp.

Clark, Robert E.D., *Darwin: Before and After* (Chicago: Moody Press, 1967), 192 pp.

Clark, Harold W., *Fossils, Flood and Fire* (Escondido, Calif.: Outdoor Pictures, 1968), 239 pp.

Cook, Melvin A., *Prehistory and Earth Models* (London: Max Parrish Co., 1966), 353 pp.

Coppedge, James, *Evolution; Possible or Impossible?* (Grand Rapids: Zondervan, 1973), 276 pp.

Cousins, Frank W., *Fossil Man* (Hants, England: Evolution Protest Movement, 1966), 106 pp.

Daly, Reginald, *Earth's Most Challenging Mysteries* (Nutley, N.J.: Craig Press, 1972), 403 pp.

Davidheiser, Bolton, *Evolution and Christian Faith* (Nutley, N.J.: Presbyterian and Reformed Publ. Co., 1969), 372 pp.

Dewar, Douglas, *The Transformist Illusion* (Murfreesboro, Tenn.: DeHoff Publ., 1955), 306 pp.

Enoch, H., *Evolution or Creation* (Madras: Union of Evangelical Students of India, 1966), 172 pp.

Friar, Wayne & Wm. P. Davis, *The Case for Creation* (Chicago: Moody Press, 1972), 93 pp.

*Gish, Duane T., *Speculations and Experiments on the Origin of Life* (San Diego: Institute for Creation Research, 1972), 41 pp.

*Gish, Duane T., *Evolution: The Fossils Say No!* (San Diego: Institute for Creation Research, 1973), 144 pp.

Klotz, John W., *Genes, Genesis and Evolution* (St. Louis: Concordia, 1970), 544 pp.

*Lammerts, W.E. (Ed.), *Why Not Creation?* (Philadelphia: Presbyterian and Reformed Co., 1970), 388 pp.

*Lammerts, W.E. (Ed.), *Scientific Studies in Special Creation* (Philadelphia: Presbyterian and Reformed Co., 1971), 343 pp.

Marsh, Frank L., *Life, Man and Time* (Escondido, Calif.: Outdoor Pictures, 1967), 238 pp.

*Moore, John N. and Harold S. Slusher (Eds.), *Biology: A Search for Order in Complexity* (2nd Edition, Grand Rapids: Zondervan, 1974), 595 pp.

*Morris, Henry M. and John C. Whitcomb, *The Genesis Flood* (Philadelphia: Presbyterian and Reformed Co., 1961), 518 pp.

*Morris, Henry M., *The Twilight of Evolution* (Grand Rapids: Baker Book House, 1964), 103 pp.

*Morris, Henry M., Wm. W. Boardman, and Robert F. Koontz, *Science and Creation* (San Diego: Creation-Science Reserch Center, 1971), 98 pp.

Morris, Henry M. et al: *A Symposium on Creation* (Grand Rapids: Baker Book House, 1968), 156 pp.

Patten, Donald W. (Ed.), *Symposium on Creation II* (Grand Rapids: Baker Book House, 1970, 151 pp.

Patten, Donald W. (Ed.), *Symposium on Creation III* (Grand Rapids: Baker Book House, 1971), 150 pp.

Patten, Donald W. (Ed.), *Symposium on Creation IV* (Grand Rapids: Baker Book House, 1972), 159 pp.

Shute, Evan, *Flaws in the Theory of Evolution* (Philadelphia: Presbyterian and Reformed Co., 1966), 286 pp.

Siegler, H.R., *Evolution or Degeneration—Which?* (Milwaukee: Northwestern Publishing House, 1972), 128 pp.

*Slusher, Harold S., *Critique of Radiometric Dating* (San Diego: Institute for Creation Research, 1973), 46 pp.

Smith, A.E. Wilder, *Man's Origin, Man's Destiny* (Wheaton, Ill.: Harold Shaw Co., 1968), 320 pp.

Smith, A.E. Wilder, *The Creation of Life* (Wheaton, Ill.: Harold Shaw Publishers, 1970), 269 pp.

Tinkle, William J., *Heredity* (Grand Rapids: Zondervan, 1970), 182 pp.

Utt, Richard H. (Ed.), *Creation: Nature's Designs and*

Designer (Mountain View, Calif.: Pacific Press, 1971), 182 pp.

Zimmerman, Paul A. (Ed.), *Darwin, Evolution and Creation* (St. Louis: Concordia, 1959), 231 pp.

II. *Books by evolutionists containing valuable critiques of aspects of evolutionary theory or practice.*

Barzun, Jacques, *Darwin, Marx, Wagner* (New York: Doubleday, 1958), 373 pp.

Blum, Harold F., *Time's Arrow and Evolution* (Princeton: Princeton University Press, 1962), 224 pp.

Haller, John S., *Outcasts From Evolution* (Urbana: University of Illinois, 1971), 228 pp.

Heribert-Nilsson, N., *Synthetische Artbildung* (An English summary) (Victoria, B.C.: Evolutionist Protest Movement, 1973).

Himmelfarb, Gertrude, *Darwin and the Darwinian Revolution* (London: Chatto and Windus, 1959), 422 pp.

Keith, Arthur, *Evolution and Ethics* (New York: Putnam, 1947), 239 pp.

Kerkut, G.A., *Implications of Evolution* (London: Pergamon Press, 1960), 174 pp.

MacBeth, Norman, *Darwin Retried* (Boston: Gambit, Inc., 1971), 172 pp.

Matthews, L. Harrison, *Introduction to "Origin of Species"* (London: J. M. Dent & Sons, Ltd., 1971).

Moorhead, P.S. and M.M. Kaplan (Eds.), *Mathematical Challenges to the Neo-Darwinian Interpretation of Evolution* (Philadelphia: Wistar Institute Press, 1967), 140 pp.

Salet, G., *Hasard et Certitude* (Paris: Tequi-Diffusion, 1972), 456 pp.

Zirkle, Conway, *Evolution, Marxian Biology, and the So-*

cial Scene (Philadelphia: University of Pennsylvania Press, 1959), 527 pp.

III. *Books by creationist authors, both scientists and theologians, discussing relation between science and the Bible.*

Clark, R. T. and James D. Bales, *Why Scientists Accept Evolution* (Nutley, N.J.: Presbyterian and Reformed Publ. Co., 1966), 113 pp.

Coder, S. Maxwell and George F. Howe, *The Bible, Science and Creation* (Chicago: Moody Press, 1965), 128 pp.

*Morris, Henry M., *Many Infallible Proofs* (San Diego: Creation-Life Publishers, 1974), 386 pp.

*Morris, Henry M., *Evolution and the Modern Christian* (Philadelphia: Presbyterian and Reformed Publ. Co., 1967), 72 pp.

*Morris, Henry M., *The Remarkable Birth of Planet Earth* (San Diego: Institute for Creation Research, 1972), 114 pp.

*Morris, Henry M., *Science, Scripture and Salvation* (Denver: Baptist Publications, 1971), 155 pp.

*Morris, Henry M., *Biblical Cosmology and Modern Science* (Nutley, N.J.: Craig Press, 1970), 146 pp.

*Morris, Henry M., *Studies in the Bible and Science* (Philadelphia: Presbyterian and Reformed Co., 1966), 186 pp.

*Morris, Henry M., *The Bible and Modern Science* (Chicago: Moody Press, 1968), 128 pp.

Nelson, Byron C., *The Deluge Story in Stone* (Minneapolis: Bethany Fellowship, 1968), 204 pp.

Rehwinkel, Alfred A., *The Flood* (St. Louis: Concordia, 1951), 372 pp.

Rushdoony, Rousas J., *The Mythology of Science* (Nutley, N.J.: Craig Press, 1967), 134 pp.

*Schnabel, A.O., *Has God Spoken?* (San Diego: Creation-Life Publishers, 1974), 118 pp.

Tinkle, William J., *God's Method in Creation* (Nutley, N.J.: Craig Press, 1973), 93 pp.

*Whitcomb, John C. *Origin of the Solar System* (Nutley, N.J.: Presbyterian and Reformed Publ. Co., 1964), 34 pp.

*Whitcomb, John C., *The Early Earth* (Nutley, N.J.: Craig Press, 1972), 144 pp.

*Whitcomb, John C., *The World That Perished* (Grand Rapids: Baker Book House, 1973), 155 pp.

*Woods, Andrew J., *The Center of the Earth* (San Diego: Institute for Creation Research, 1973), 18 pp.

* Available from Creation-Life Publishers, P.O. Box 15666, San Diego, CA 92115.

Recommended Periodicals:

Acts and Facts (San Diego, Institute for Creation Research, published monthly).

Creation Research Quarterly (Ann Arbor, Michigan, Creation Research Society, published quarterly).

Doorway Papers (Ottawa, Arthur C. Custance, published as ready).

Bible-Science Newsletter (Minneapolis, Bible-Science Association, published monthly).

E.P.M. Papers (Hayling Island, Hants, England, Evolution Protest Movement, published as ready).

Other Books on Creationism:

Morris, Henry M., Ed., *Scientific Creationism* (San Diego: Creation-Life Publishers, 1974).

Rimmer, Harry, *Dead Men Tell Tales* (Grand Rapids: Eerdmans, 1939).

Rimmer, Harry, *The Harmony of Science and Scripture* (Grand
Rapids: Eerdmans, 1936).

Rimmer, Harry, *The Magnificence of Jesus* (Grand Rapids:
Eerdmans, 1943).

Rimmer, Harry, *Modern Science and the Genesis Record*
(Grand Rapids: Eerdmans, 1937).

Rimmer, Harry, *Theory of Evolution and the Facts of Science*
(Grand Rapids: Eerdmans, 1935).

Other Helpful Publications for Bible Believers:

The Bible Science Association, 2911 East 42nd Street, Minneapolis, MN 55406, has published the following bulletins or
tracts on special aspects of creationism:

Psalms 19:1: *The Heavens Declare the Glory of God.*

Job 40:15–24: *The Dinosaur and Human Footprints Together.*

Isaiah 34:16, Matthew 5:9: *Remarkable Accuracy of Bible
Dates.*

Jeremiah 31:28: *Cyclic Interpretation of History.*

Proverbs 1:7: *How Creation Improves Education.*

Psalms 46:2: *The Rise of Catastrophism in Geology.*

Genesis 7:11–24: *How Creationists Are Turning Cellulose into
Fuel.*

Genesis 1:11–12: *The Pine Pollen Debate.*

Psalms 102:26: *The Decay of the Earth's Magnetic Field.*

Job 38:4, 6: *Pleochroic Halos Demand Created Basement
Rocks.*

Romans 1:20: *The Mixing Problem in Radiometric Dating.*

Colossians 1:16: *Rise of Creation Evangelism.*

Footnotes

Chapter 1

1. Even Darwin knew he could not prove his theory. In 1863, he wrote, "When we descend to details, we can prove that no one species has changed [i.e., we cannot prove that any one species has changed]; nor can we prove that the supposed changes are beneficial, which is the groundwork of the theory. Nor can we explain why some species have changed and others have not." (As quoted on page 419 of *Darwin and the Darwinian Revolution,* by Gertrude Himmelfarb, Garden City, NY: Doubleday, 1959.)

Chapter 4

1. Jews call Jesus by His Hebrew name, Yeshua. He is the Messiah spoken of by the prophets in the Tenach, the Hebrew Bible.
2. As reported by Dr. D. Lee Chesnut, in "The Atom Speaks" and other papers (Minneapolis, Minn.: Bible-Science Association).
3. Raising your eyebrows and asking, "But what about heavy water?" Yes, there is such a thing, but it doesn't wreck our argument. Heavy water is made from a heavy isotope of hydrogen called deuterium (chemical symbol D). The formula is D_2O. And

because heavy water makes up only about one part in 5,000 parts of ordinary water, its contrary properties don't run the show.

Chapter 5

1. The remarkable cell even contains a special mechanism for self-destruction when the right time comes. The mechanism goes into operation the moment life departs, accelerating the cell's rate of oxidation to ensure speedy decay of the dead body. Once the death certificate is signed, you might say, decay is given the green light to get on with its job of making room for "live ones."
2. Graham Berry, "Life Shaped to Order," *Modern Maturity*, December, 1983, p. 65.

Chapter 6

1. Unless otherwise indicated, quotations in this chapter are adapted from "Voices of Science on Evolution," by Prof. Robert Whitelaw, Civil Engineering Department, Virginia Polytechnic Institute, Blacksburg, Virginia, as it appeared in the *Bible-Science Newsletter* for August-September, 1972, pages 8, 9, 11, and from Ray Smith's article, "The Folly of Evolution," in the August-September, 1974, issue of the *Bible-Science Newsletter*.
2. Ray Smith, "The Folly of Evolution." *The Bible Science Newsletter*, August-September, 1974.
3. The Greek for "science" in this verse is *gnosis*. It refers, most likely, to gnostic religion, a first-century heresy akin to Christian Science. Whenever "science" goes to origins, it goes to gnosticism, because the origin of things is neither repeatable nor observable—therefore, if it is called "science," it is falsely so called.

Chapter 12

1. Heard on BBC shortwave broadcast direct from Jodrell Bank Observatory in England, reporting their huge radiotelescope reception of "intelligent radio messages incapable of being deciphered at our present state of intelligence."

Appendix IV

1. Stager, Lawrence E. and Samuel R. Wolff, "Child Sacrifice at Carthage," *Biblical Archaeology Review,* Vol. X, No. 1, January/February, 1984, p. 33.